CLERGY DISSENT

IN THE

OLD SOUTH,

1830–1865

CLERGY DISSENT

IN THE

OLD SOUTH,

1830–1865

David B. Chesebrough

Southern Illinois University Press
Carbondale and Edwardsville

Library of Congress Cataloging-in-Publication Data

Chesebrough, David B., 1932–
    Clergy dissent in the Old South, 1830–1865 / David B.
Chesebrough.
        p.   cm.
    Includes bibliographical references and index.
    1. Slavery and the church—Southern States—History—
19th century. 2. Clergy—Southern States—Political activity—
History—19th century.   3. Dissenters—Southern States—
History—19th century.   4. Southern States—History—1775–
1865.   5. Confederate States of America—History.   I. Title.
    E449.C523   1996
    975'.03—dc20   96-7669
    ISBN 0-8093-2080-0 (alk. paper)   CIP

The paper used in this publication meets the minimum
requirements of American National Standard for
Information Sciences—Permanence of Paper for Printed
Library Materials, ANSI Z39.48-1984. ∞

For
Arlan G. Richardson,
a treasured friend whose encouragement
led to my academic career

Contents

Illustrations

Preface

During the antebellum and war years in the southern states of America, enormous pressures were exerted upon its citizens to produce universal conformity, first, for slavery, and, then, for secession and war. Though the South made impressive progress toward such a goal, unanimity, of course, could never be achieved. There were always those who dissented. This dissension has been explored in two important books: Georgia Lee Tatum's *Disloyalty in the Confederacy* (1934) and Carl N. Degler's *The Other South: Southern Dissenters in the Nineteenth Century* (1974).

This work focuses on a particular type of southern dissent, specifically, that which emanated from the clergy. From 1830 to 1860, the issue of slavery dominated, but from late 1860 on, secession and war emerged as major concerns. The geographical boundaries under observation include the eleven states of the Confederacy, plus the border state of Kentucky. Kentucky is included because dissent on slavery in that state was, as will be shown, a very serious matter. Also included is one incident in Washington, D.C., which demonstrates how unpopular it was, even in the nation's capital, for a member of the clergy to attack the institution of slavery.

The number or the percentage of dissenting clergy in the South will never be known, even as the number of dissenters in the general population cannot be determined. We do know, however, that the number and percentage of dissident clergy in the upper South was greater than in the lower South. This trend can also be found in the general population. There were areas in the upper South, such as western Virginia and eastern Tennessee, that contained much support for the Union during the war. Yet, even in these areas, it will be noted, there was a price to be paid for dissent. One must look harder to find the record of dissidents in the lower South, but the findings are worth the extra effort. Their stories are more dramatic and their punishments more severe, often resulting in imprisonment and sometimes in death. All of the clergy members referred to in this work are Protestants who represented over 95 percent of the churches in the South during this era. As will be developed in chapter 1, it was the Protestants, their clergy, and denominational presses, who in large measure helped to shape and reinforce the southern agenda. Therefore, the dissenters mentioned are limited to this group.

Chapter 1, "The Stance of the Majority," is a brief overview of the role most of the southern clergy played in the antebellum and war years, supporting, like the vast majority of white Southerners, slavery, secession, and war. The clergy were in the forefront of those who justified slavery and called for secession. From the beginning, they could be found among the most ardent supporters of the war and could be counted among the last to concede defeat.

Chapter 2, "The Winnowing Years, 1830–1861," is an account of those years when much of the South attempted to portray a united front in support of slavery and earnest attempts were made to stifle dissent. The clergy who would not support the "peculiar institution" either kept their silence, moved to the North, or suffered various consequences for dissenting.

Chapter 3, "The War Years, 1861–1865," introduces two more issues over which dissent arose: secession from the Union and the war to secure the right to establish a new nation. Some clergy who formally supported and justified slavery could not support secession and war. To dissent over these latter issues, however, was to invite the label of *traitor*, and the consequences of such dissension were often even more severe than those suffered by opponents of slavery.

In the conclusion of this work, "The Creative Minority," emphasis is placed upon the necessary and important role that dissenters play in any society, the extent to which dissenters often perceive events more clearly than the majority, and the way in which, over time, dissenters are often proved right and in advance of their times. A question raised in this chapter is whether the clergy mold or reflect society. An attempt is made to find a common thread among the dissenting clergy in the South, and an inquiry is made as to why a few of these dissenters were able to hold onto their positions throughout the war.

Acknowledgments

It would be difficult to publicly acknowledge all of those who have been so helpful in the publication of this book, but it is imperative that a few be cited. First on my list would be the personnel of Southern Illinois University Press. Through the various stages of production, the people associated with the Press have been both helpful and encouraging. Thomas Connors, a colleague at Illinois State University, read portions of the manuscript and offered his insightful counsel.

During the preparation of this work, I submitted material on clergy dissent in Mississippi to *The Journal of Mississippi History*. For suggestions offered by the editors and the eventual publication of an article on this topic, I am indebted.

Most of all, to Sharon Hagan Foiles, who, as with previous books, was such a big help in producing a manuscript that was readable and usable, my deepest appreciation.

CLERGY DISSENT

IN THE

OLD SOUTH,

1830–1865

One

The Stance of the Majority

THE VITAL ROLE played by southern clergy in the defense of slavery and the ensuing calls for a separate southern nation, even at the cost of war, have been well documented and noted. Historian James W. Silver has written: "Clergymen led the way to secession. . . . As no other group, Southern clergymen were responsible for a state of mind which made secession possible, and as no other group they sustained the people in their long, costly, and futile War for Southern Independence." In *Gospel of Disunion: Religion and Separatism in the Antebellum South,* Mitchell Snay affirms "that religion played a major role in the formation of a Southern national identity. . . . Southern ministers invested the sectional conflict with religious significance." Emory M. Thomas has suggested that "perhaps Southern churches are the best place to look for the origins of cultural nationalism in the Old South." Another historian has declared that "among the institutions within the Confederate States of America, none did more than the churches to further the Southern cause. Through their personal example and their sermons, the clergy were able to exert pressure upon the conduct of their followers." Yet another historian has emphasized that "clergymen were second to no other professional class in buttressing the struggle for southern independence."[1]

Similar observations have been drawn not just by later observers, but by those who lived during the sectional crisis. William G. Brownlow, a pro-Union Methodist minis-

ter and newspaper editor from Tennessee, in the spring of
1861, about one month after the firing on Fort Sumter,
accused that "the clergy of the South—without distinction
of sects—men of talents, learning, and influence—have
raised the howl of Secession, and it falls like an Indian war-
cry upon our citizens from their prostituted pulpits every
Sabbath." From the border state of Kentucky, as the war
was nearing its end, former pastor and then professor of
practical theology at the Theological Seminary of the Presbyterian Church at Danville, Robert Livingston Stanton,
wrote of the commonly held perception as to the southern
clergy's responsibility for the sectional conflict. "Politicians, secular and religious journals, pamphleteers, men in
all classes of society," he wrote, "freely lay the blame of this
Rebellion, in great measure, or wholly, at the door of the
Church; charging the ministry, more especially, with having caused it. This is a very prevalent sentiment."[2]

A great contribution of the churches and clergy to
the sundering of the nation may well have been the schisms
of the Presbyterian, Methodist, and Baptist denominations
in 1837, 1844, and 1845, respectively. These three denominations, at the commencement of the Civil War, represented 94 percent of the churches in the South: the
Methodists with 45 percent, the Baptists with 37 percent,
and the Presbyterians with 12 percent. C. C. Goen has
claimed that the schisms in the three denominations at least
fifteen years before the war provided a model and an inspi-
ration for later political division. "The denominational
schisms," he wrote, "as irreversible steps along the nation's
tortuous course to violence, were both portent and cata-
lyst to the imminent national tragedy." Elaborating upon
the churches' contribution to divisiveness, Goen continued: "They broke a bond of national unity, encouraged
the myth of 'peaceable secession,' established a precedent
of sectional independence, reinforced the growing alien-
ation between the North and South by cultivating distorted
images of 'the other side,' and exacerbated the moral outrage that each section felt against the other." Goen be-

lieves that the clergy were cognizant of the far-reaching and devastating consequences their actions would have. "The leaders of the dividing churches," he accused, "were aware of the probable political consequences of what they were doing, and that even so dismal a prospect as the ruin of their cherished political union did not deter them."[3]

Other historians have made similar evaluations. William Warren Sweet has written: "There are good arguments to support the claim that the split in the churches was not only the first break between the sections, but the chief cause of the final break." Allen Nevins, in his comprehensive account of the Civil War, stated that "the divided churches had contributed significantly to the [political] estrangement." Charles S. Sydnor has set forth the important role of the denominational schisms in pushing the nation forward to irreparable differences.

> The division of the churches was something more than an ecclesiastical event. The churches were among the great cohesive forces in America, serving along with the Whig and Democratic parties, business organizations, and other institutions to reinforce the Federal government in the maintenance of the American union. The snapping of any one of these bonds under the stress of sectional tension inevitably increased the strain upon the others. The churches were the first to break; and when they did, tension upon the other national organizations was brought nearer to the danger point.[4]

The first denominational rupture took place in 1837, when the Presbyterian Church in the U.S.A. divided between the Old School (those with great reservations about revivalism) and the New School (those enthusiastic about revivalistic activities). Though the break was not strictly a North-South division, most Southerners tended to side with the Old School. A powerful reason for this was that Southerners saw an alarming amount of abolitionist activity in the New School. When the Presbyterian General Assembly assured Southerners that discussion of slavery would cease, Southerners voted with the Old School to purge the New School synods from their midst. The presbyteries in the South that at first sided with the New School came over to the Old School in 1857, no longer able to endure the influence of abolitionism, and the North-South division of the Presbyterian denomination was complete.

The Methodists expressed their disapproval of slavery in 1784 when the denomination was formally organized in America. However, no national rules were ever enforced, and slavery became a local option. Abolitionists in the North began forcing the issue. In 1843, there was a large defection of antislavery Methodists who organized the Wesleyan Methodist Church. The next year the General Conference voted that a southern bishop, James O. Andrew, could no longer hold his office because he owned slaves. The Southerners withdrew from the denomination and the following year established the Methodist Episcopal Church, South, as a proslavery denomination.

The national Baptists, who were loosely organized around societies and boards for missionary purposes, divided in 1845, one year after the Methodist schism. In that year, Alabama Baptists asked the Foreign Mission Board if it would appoint a slaveholder for missionary service. After struggling to find a way around the dilemma, the board responded negatively. Baptists from the South withdrew and formed the Southern Baptist Convention, a Baptist denomination more tightly organized than anything Baptists, who prided themselves on adherence to local autonomy, had ever experienced in their history.

Contemporaries well understood the serious implications of the denominational ruptures. In 1845, Tennessee Methodist William C. Booth spoke of the national danger posed by the Methodist schism. "It has in truth," he said, "been already hailed as the harbinger of disunion." Late in the same year, an Alabama Baptist wrote: "Let the three great religious denominations, the Presbyterian, the Methodist, and the Baptist, declare off from union effort to do good, North and South, and our glorious union of States will be greatly weakened, if not sundered entirely." The South Carolina Baptist Convention asked: "If we, who profess to have but one Lord, one faith, one baptism, one God and Father, cannot remain united in the cause of benevolent effort, how can they be expected to perpetuate their union on mere political principles?"[5]

The politicians also noted the threat to political union raised by the ecclesiastical schisms. In March 1850, a speech written by John C. Calhoun was delivered before the United States Senate. Too feeble and weak to deliver the speech himself, Calhoun had it delivered by another. The speech began by recognizing the importance of religious cords in binding the nation together. "The cords that bind the States together," wrote Calhoun, "are not only many but various in character. . . . The strongest of those of spiritual and ecclesiastical nature, consisted in the unity of the great religious denominations, all of which embraced the whole union." Taking note that the religious cords had snapped—he singled out the Methodists and Baptists as points of focus—Calhoun warned of what would happen if the turmoil continued. "If the agitation goes on," he cautioned, "the same force, acting with increased intensity, as has been shown, will finally snap every cord, when nothing will be left to hold the States together except force." Two years later, Henry Clay raised a similar concern. "I tell you," he exclaimed, "this sundering of religious ties which have hitherto bound our people together, I consider the greatest source of danger to our country. If our religious men cannot live together in peace, what can be expected of us politicians, very few of whom profess to be governed by the great principles of love?"[6]

Many southern clergy and the various religious institutions of which they were a part issued calls for the southern states to secede from the Union and form a separate nation before secession actually took place. James W. Silver has noted several examples of preachers calling for their states to secede from the Union. "Thomas Caskey," he recorded, "minister of the Christian Church in Jackson, set out with the Attorney General of Mississippi to 'talk the people out of the Union.' Bishop Francis H. Rutledge promised to pay into the Florida treasury, five hundred dollars when the state seceded." After Lincoln's election, denominations joined individuals in demanding political division: "North Carolina Presbyterians, professing to speak for four-fifths of the Southern clergy and church members, called on all the slave states to make common cause. . . . The Alabama, Mississippi, and South Carolina Baptists officially considered it the duty of their states to secede immediately."[7]

Early in November 1860, a few days after the election of Abraham Lincoln to the presidency, the Alabama Baptist State Convention, proclaimed their state's "right, as a sovereignty, to withdraw from the Union." One month before Georgia seceded, the Methodist Conference in the state voted eighty-seven to nine in favor of secession. Religious publications joined the call for separation. On January 3, 1861, the *Mississippi Baptist* proclaimed: "The separation of these States from the Federal Union is a political necessity and must be effected at any cost, regardless of consequences." The *Southern Episcopalian* of Charleston declared that secession was "the only position that Southern freemen or Southern Christians can consistently occupy." Historian David Potter has summarized that "clergymen from the pulpit were almost as vocal as politicians from the stump in warning of the dangers to the South, exhorting the people to declare their independence, and keeping emotions at a high pitch."[8]

Slavery was the issue that caused southern clerics to become ardent proponents of southern nationalism, that transformed a political issue into a religious one with significant moral overtones. In the eighteenth century, most southern evangelical clergy members—basically Methodists, Baptists, and Presbyterians—were opposed to slavery. In 1784, the Methodists passed a series of strict rules for the purpose of eliminating slavery from their churches. In

1790, the Virginia General Committee (Baptist) declared slavery to be "a violent deprivation of the rights of nature and inconsistent with a republican government" and urged "every legal measure to extirpate the horrid evil from the land." It needs to be noted, however, that many Virginia Baptists did not receive the committee's declaration favorably.[9] It was typical in the eighteenth century for southern churches, denominations, and clergy to take antislavery stances with which many in their constituencies did not agree.

About the turn of the century and for the first two decades of the new century, as slavery became more and more identified with the southern way of life, southern ecclesiastical organizations, clergy, and religious periodicals began to a adopt a stance of silence on the slavery issue. Retreating from earlier antislavery positions, the southern clergy began to affirm that slavery was a civil matter and not a religious concern. This position, sometimes called "the spirituality of the church," is thought to have been introduced by Presbyterians in the South, but it became the position adopted by most southern Christians. Writing of this period, Eugene D. Genovese comments that the southern clergy who increasingly believed "that the Bible sanctioned slavery" came to the conclusion that slavery "was strictly a civil, a political question on which the church could take no position."[10] Donald G. Matthews has written that a kind of litany was developed which described the ecclesiastical silence on the slavery issue.

> Slaveholding is a civil institution:
> and we [churches and clergy] will not interfere.
> The character of civil institutions is governed by politics; and we will not interfere.
> Politics are beyond the scope of the church;
> and we will not interfere.[11]

In the 1830s, most southern clergy once again changed their stance on the slavery issue. By the beginning of the fourth decade of the nineteenth century, the overwhelming majority of southern clergy were ardently and defiantly defending the "peculiar institution." The churches and their ministers were numbered among the South's most vociferous proponents of slavery.

What happened in the 1830s that caused the southern preachers to become such passionate defenders of slavery? It will be recalled that in August 1831, a fanatical, visionary slave preacher, Nat Turner, led a slave uprising that resulted in the slaughter of about sixty white Virginians, mostly women and children. It was not lost upon the southern populace that at the beginning of the same year William Lloyd Garrison, in Boston, had published the first edition of the *Liberator*, which demanded immediate emancipation of the slaves. "I will be as harsh as truth," wrote Garrison. "On this subject [slavery] I do not wish to think, or speak, or write with moderation. . . . I am in earnest—I will not equivocate—I will not excuse—I will not retreat a single inch." That Garrison's demands and the Turner revolt were related, the South had no doubts. Northern abolitionism was perceived as a dangerous threat to the southern way of life, most especially the institution of slavery. Church historian Sydney E. Ahlstrom has noted that Garrison "did far more than any other man to heighten Southern opposition to emancipation."[12]

Most importantly for the southern clergy, and the chief factor that brought them into the sectional controversy, was that they perceived abolitionism as inseparably intertwined with northern religion. Overlooked was the fact that in the 1830s, many, perhaps most, northern ministers were opposed to the abolitionist movement, viewing it as disruptive, divisive, and radical. On October 17, 1833, Joseph Tracy delivered a sermon, which was one of the earliest clerical attacks upon the abolitionists, before the Vermont Colonization Society. The following year, Simon Clough, a Congregational minister from Fall River, Massachusetts, preached a sermon in which he denounced the abolitionists as being antibiblical. He suggested that preach-

ers who espoused abolitionist principles be dismissed by
their congregations as false teachers. In 1839, Horace
Bushnell from Connecticut, in a sermon that was a response
to the abolitionists, warned against hasty antislavery actions
and urged that southern men be given time to correct the
abuses of slavery through gradual legislative action. In the
next decade, though their numbers were fewer, several
northern clergymen could still be found who were casti-
gating the abolitionists. George Junkin, in 1843, before
the Synod of Cincinnati (Old School Presbyterian), delivered an eight-hour attack upon abolitionism. One year
later, Charles Porter from Utica, New York, urged his listeners to reject insurrectionary efforts (abolitionism) that
were tearing America apart and thus were a greater evil
than slavery. To such charges, Garrison complained: "I
have been almost as cruelly opposed by ministers of the
Gospel and church members as by any other class of men."
By the late 1850s, most northern clergy were generally sup-
portive of abolitionism, but the process had been slow and
gradual.[13]

In spite of vigorous opposition to abolitionists by many
of the northern clergy, especially in the 1830s and early
1840s, the southern clergy, nevertheless, generalized that
abolitionism was a movement based upon and motivated
by a perverted northern religion. Snay has observed that
"although Southern clerics recognized that the conservative clergy of the North opposed abolitionism, they none-
theless remained haunted by the intimacy between religion
and the attack on slavery. . . . Southern ministers portrayed
abolitionism as a fanatical crusade that wantonly politicized
and perverted religion." In 1836, a Methodist newspaper,
the *Virginia Conference Sentinel,* accused that abolitionism "derives its whole strength from the religious influence
of the North. It is to all intents and purposes a question of
religion." The Reverend James Henley Thornwell, by many
standards a moderate South Carolina Presbyterian, proclaimed "the confrontation with abolitionists as one between a Christian people and the Antichrist."[14]

The southern ministers, in their attempts to protect and defend the institution of slavery against the charges from a heretical North, turned to their Bibles where they "discovered" that slavery was a God-ordained, biblically sanctioned way of life. Theodore Clapp, in an 1838 sermon at the First Congregational Church in New Orleans, spoke of the transformation in his own life on the subject of slavery, a transformation experienced by several southern clerics. He related that after many years of uncertainty, and even involvement in emancipation schemes, he was at last "fully convinced of the rectitude of slavery." According to Clapp, the most significant factor for this revolutionary change was his study of the Scriptures. In 1837, Samuel Dunwoody, a Methodist minister from South Carolina, claimed that God, in the Bible made provision for perpetual slavery. The Negro race, he insisted, was condemned to an existence in slavery. In 1844, W. T. Hamilton, from Alabama, delivered a sermon, "Duties of Masters and Slaves Respectively; or, Domestic Slavery as Sanctioned by the Bible," in which he denounced abolitionists as antislavery radicals, sinners who should be denied communion with other Christians. Hundreds, more likely thousands, of sermons with similar themes were delivered throughout the South in response to an abolitionist-religious challenge. The passionate defense of slavery continued on through the end of the war, after which the argument changed a bit in order to justify, sanctify, and legitimize segregation.[15]

A subtheme the southern preachers found in their Bibles to further justify slavery was the doctrine of racial inequality. This doctrine held that those of the black race were inferior to those of the white race, a concept the preachers believed was supported through the biblical stories of the curse of Ham and/or the punishment of Cain.[16]

Doctrines of natural rights and the concept that all men are created equal were anathema to most southern clergy. In late 1844 and early 1845, the Reverend Richard Fuller, a Southern Baptist minister from South Carolina, and the Reverend Francis Wayland, a Baptist clergyman from the North, wrote a series of letters to each other on the subject of slavery. Fuller defended the institution; Wayland opposed it. In one of his letters, Fuller, a moderate man by many standards, challenged the idea of natural rights as an argument against slavery. "Government is restraint," he asserted; "the very idea of government includes an abridgement of that personal freedom which a savage has in the forest." Fuller then asked: "Is it, then, necessarily a crime for a government to discriminate between those whom it controls, in the distribution of civil privileges and political liberty? It surely would be preposterous to affirm this." Fuller continued: "Every government . . . has a right . . . to establish those regulations which shall best promote the good of the whole population."[17]

Other clergy were even more emphatic than Fuller. One said that it was a fallacious concept that held that "all men, simply from the fact of being men, have a natural right to an equal amount of property, or an equal share of personal liberty." People were placed in different circumstances and social relations "under the providence of God." Therefore, "some are rulers, some subjects; some are rich, some poor; some are fathers, some children; some are bond, some free. And if a man is justly and providentially a ruler, he has the rights of a father; and if a slave, only the rights of a slave."[18] It was an order that God had ordained.

Matthews makes the point that many southern evangelical preachers, in their desire to establish the doctrine of human inequality,

> insulted and demeaned a majority of their own constituency with the same . . . insensitivity which they usually reserved for talking about black people. In tract upon tract, male writers emphasized the subordination of women as built into the very nature of human society by God himself, citing Scripture to that effect and rewarding the submissiveness of women with elaborate praise for her grace, "passive fortitude," and "enduring love."[19]

Matthews then cites the declaration of Frederick Ross, a Presbyterian minister from Huntsville, Alabama, who bound together the subservient positions of slaves and women. "Do you say," asked Ross, "the slave is held to involuntary service? So is the wife. Her relation to her husband, in the immense majority of cases, is made for her, and not by her." He reminded the wives that they, like the slaves, were "under service," and "bound to obey their husbands." Ross continued: "Do you say the slave is sold and bought? So is the wife the world over."[20] Ross, along with many other southern clergy, spoke and wrote about the inequality of women to justify their stances on the inequality of Blacks.

There were many ways, the preachers asserted, in which those of the black race were different from those of the white race. There were anatomical and physiological differences. It was generally held that Blacks were less intelligent and more emotional than Whites. They were also supposed to be more sensual and superstitious, less disciplined and less orderly. One had only to look at human behavior in Africa, the original habitat of Blacks, clerics reminded, to become aware of how different in culture, values, and social mores the Blacks were from Whites: Africans conducted human sacrifices, ate one another, and "worshipped the devil, practiced witchcraft, and sorcery, disregarded the marriage rites, murdered, swore false, practiced all kinds of dissimulation."[21]

Because southern ministers perceived the abolitionist attack on slavery as motivated by unorthodox religion, the defense of slavery became a part of a much larger picture. The argument was more than proslavery versus antislavery; it was a struggle between true religion and false religion, between orthodoxy and heresy, and between a biblically revealed religion and a man-made religion. Those who opposed the biblically sanctioned and God-ordained institution were in effect anti-God and anti-Bible. Thus, the North in general, and the abolitionists in particular, were castigated as heretics and infidels. In 1850, James Henley

Thornwell, an eminent South Carolina preacher, publisher, and educator, who was often referred to as the "Calhoun of the Church," delivered a sermon, "The Rights and the Duties of Masters," which still stands as one of the classic biblical, social, and political defenses of slavery. Throughout the sermon, Thornwell sought to answer the various charges being made by northern abolitionists that slavery was immoral and contrary to the spirit of the Gospel. He argued that slavery was not inconsistent with personal rights and moral obligations. Drawing a distinction between a man and his labor, Thornwell contended that though a master owned another's labor, he really did not own the laborer. It was in the very early sentences that the clergyman drew the larger perspective. "The parties in this conflict," he emphasized, "are not merely abolitionists and slaveholders—they are atheists, socialists, communists, red republicans, jacobins, on the one side, and friends of order and regulated freedom on the other. In one word, the world is the battleground—Christianity and Atheism the combatants; and the progress of humanity the stake."[22]

During the war years, Isaac T. Tichenor, pastor of the First Baptist Church in Montgomery, Alabama, delivered an address before the General Assembly of the State of Alabama. In the address, he summarized the biblical foundations of slavery. "That slavery is sanctioned by the Bible," he announced, "seems scarcely to admit of doubt. Founded upon the divine decree that 'Canaan should be a servant of servants unto his brethren,' existing in the days of the patriarchs, twice spoken of in the ten commandments, with laws written in the New Testament for its regulation, it stands as an institution of God." Tichenor, therefore, denounced the North because it demanded "an anti-slavery Constitution, an anti-slavery Bible, and an anti-slavery God." According to numerous southern clergy, the North was inferior and debased, a den of iniquity where law and order had broken down. Mob rule, such as abolitionism, was everywhere rampant. Basic to the cultural breakdown in the North was a decline in true and orthodox religion. A southern religious journal declared:

> Our Societies [southern] enjoy profound tranquility so
> far as doctrinal speculations or pseudo reform of organic
> principles are concerned. We are not troubled—as they
> are in New England, with Mormonism, Millerism,
> Comeouterism, Universalism, or with an American
> edition of German Rationalism. The Southern States are
> not the soil on which such absurdities flourish.

Snay concludes that "the biblical justification of human bondage was the most tangible contribution religion
made to the Southern cause. . . . The justification of slavery
based on the Bible and natural law and the portrayal of
abolitionism as infidelity were perhaps the most viable and
influential contributions religion made to the cause of
Southern separatism."[23]

In the decades prior to the 1830s, the southern clergy
attempted to avoid becoming involved in political and civil
matters. Caesar had his due and God had his, and it was
seldom justified to merge the two. Only if moral issues
were involved in the civil arena did the clergy feel that religious interference was warranted. Morality was the test
that determined clerical involvement in politics. For this
reason, the clergy did not become involved in the South
Carolina nullification issue of the late 1820s and early 1830s.
Though it was—especially for South Carolina and a few
other southern states that were closely observing—the most
explosive and passionate domestic political matter in many
years, it was, nevertheless, primarily a political issue and
the southern churches and clergy, for the most part, did
not become involved. As they perceived that crisis, it was a
political one with too few moral and religious overtones to
become embroiled in the controversy. The slavery issue
was a different matter, however, made so by northern abolitionists who used religion to denounce slavery as immoral
and inhumane. Religious and ethical challenges could only
be countered with religious and ethical responses. Thus,

the southern clergy saw themselves as called upon to not only defend slavery, but the Bible, God, and a divinely ordered way of life.

When it came time to call for secession and a separate southern nation, it was once again an issue fraught with moral and religious implications; thus, the consequent heavy involvement by the southern clergy. These ministers drew upon the historic millennial vision that Americans had long cherished for their nation. The early colonies, and later the new nation, were the New Israel, "a city upon a hill," God's special and chosen people, called by Divine Providence to be an example of righteousness to all humankind, the disseminator of Truth, and a redeemer nation through whom the world would find its way to God. It was a high, holy, and exclusive calling, a calling whose standards must be met, lest God's hand be removed and laid upon some other people. The southern clergy feared that Northerners, by their wickedness and infidelity, were forfeiting the nation's right to be God's chosen people and the leaders through whom the millennium would come.

The southern preachers spared no words in depicting the wretched condition of the North. William O. Prentiss, at St. Peter's Church in Charleston, South Carolina, on November 21, 1860, declared that northern society was "corrupted in its very root and principle." The following week, Andrew H. H. Boyd, in Winchester, Virginia, looked to the North and lamented that "streams of moral desolation are flowing through some portions of the country." In a sermon delivered in January 1861, some three months before the war commenced, Edwin T. Winkler referred to Northerners as "a hostile people . . . perverted in tyranny." The theme of northern wickedness was one the southern clergy continued to press throughout the war: the people of the Confederacy must never forget the terrible wickedness of the enemy they were fighting. George Foster Pierce, a Methodist bishop from Georgia, in the spring of 1863 delivered a sermon in which he drew a sharp contrast between what he perceived as the wicked North

and the God-fearing South. "We are fighting," he proclaimed, "against robbery and lust and rapine; against ruth-
less invasion, a treacherous despotism, the blight of its own
land, and the scorn of the world. . . . The triumph of our
arms is the triumph of right and truth and justice. The
defeat of our enemies is the defeat of wrong, malice and
outrage."[24]

Because the North was perverse and had destroyed
any chance the United States had for becoming the New
Israel, it was imperative for the South to break away in order to preserve its own purity and so that the millennial
vision could be carried on through a new and cleansed nation. One month before South Carolina seceded, William
O. Prentiss emphasized: "We cannot coalesce with men
whose society will eventually corrupt our own, and bring
down upon us the awful doom which awaits them." A few
months later, in Mobile, Alabama, H. N. Pierce, contem-
plating the spread of northern corruption, implored the
South not to "give up this fair land to degradation and
infamy; we cannot permit our churches and our schools . . .
our temples of justice, to be swept into common ruin."
The first official secessionist resolution to be passed by an
ecclesiastical assembly in the South was issued by the Alabama Baptist State Convention, which met November 9
through 13, 1860, about a week after Lincoln's election.
The resolution, written and proposed by Dr. Basil Manley,
said in part:

> At a moment when grave and serious issues face the
> country . . . we have the profound conviction that the
> Union of the states has failed . . . we can no longer hope
> for justice, protection or safety from the Federal Union
> . . . . We hold ourselves subject to the call of proper
> authority in defense of the sovereignty and independence
> of the State of Alabama and of her right, as a sovereignty
> to withdraw from the Union; and to make arrangements
> for securing her rights.[25]

The southern ministers often turned to the analogy of disease and death to describe the sick-unto-death North and declared the necessity of separating the healthy from the diseased lest the healthy also become infected. In March 1861, the *Southern Presbyterian* asked, "Have we not done well to cut the bonds that bound us to the body of death?" Two months earlier, Thomas Atkinson, in Wilmington, North Carolina, affirmed that God would not "permit a decaying body, out of which the life and spirit are gone, a mere carcass, to taint the atmosphere, to spread disease and death around it, but He will cause it to be removed, and He has provided instruments for the work . . . to tear in pieces, and take out of the way, any such dead and corrupting body." In light of such statements, it is little wonder that Thomas R. R. Cobb, a Confederate government official, exclaimed: "This revolution has been accomplished mainly by the Churches."[26]

In the minds and hopes of the southern clergy, secession would transfer to the Confederacy the high and holy mission of carrying the millennial torch. "It would be a glorious sight," observed the *Southern Presbyterian*, "to see this Southern Confederacy of ours stepping forth amid the nations of the world animated with a Christian spirit, guided by Christian principles, administered by Christian men, and adhering faithfully to Christian precepts." In May 1861, the Baptist Special Committee on the State of the Country emphasized that the administration of Jefferson Davis was "contributing to the transcendent Kingdom of our Lord Jesus Christ." In 1863, Presbyterian Joseph Stiles joined together the South's mission and the coming millennium. God would bring in the millennium by plucking "some one nation out of the ranks of the world to take ground for God and man under the ranks of the Gospel." Stiles was certain that chosen nation would be the Confederacy.[27]

The millennium, most southern preachers assured, would have a place for slavery. Three months prior to the war, Joseph R. Wilson, in a sermon delivered at the First

Presbyterian Church of Augusta, Georgia, projected a millennialistic view of the future in which a prominent feature would be "the institution of domestic slavery, freed from its stupid servility on the one side and its excess of neglect and severity on the other," acclaimed by all as a blessing to masters and slaves. A Presbyterian minister from Georgia prophesied that twenty years after a Confederate victory, "abolitionist individual-rights ideas would vanish from the world, and slavery, stronger than ever in the South, would flourish also in many Northern states and foreign countries."[28]

On November 29, 1860, Benjamin Morgan Palmer delivered a sermon from his prestigious pulpit at the First Presbyterian Church in New Orleans. The sermon, "Slavery a Divine Trust: Duty of the South to Preserve and Protect It," is perhaps the finest example of southern ecclesiastical rhetoric as to how the defense of slavery led to the call for secession. No preacher in the South equaled Palmer in his denunciations of the North, his defense of slavery and the southern way of life, and his advocacy of separation from the Union. James Silver has written: "Benjamin Palmer ranged up and down the country during the whole of the war, assuming the appearance of a prophet of the Lord. A general in Mississippi declared Palmer to be worth a thousand soldiers to the cause."[29] Palmer had held Presbyterian pastorates in Savannah, Georgia, and Columbia, South Carolina, before becoming the minister of the First Presbyterian Church in New Orleans in 1854, a position he held until his death in 1902. Twice during the war years, upon the approach of Union troops, Palmer had to flee, knowing that his outspokenness had made him a marked man. In the spring of 1862, he fled from New Orleans before forces led by Commodore David G. Farragut, and less than three years later, he fled from Columbia, South Carolina, as Sherman's forces drew near.

The precise dating of this 1860 sermon is important. Secession for South Carolina was three weeks away, and for Louisiana, Palmer's state, the withdrawal from the Union was yet two months into the future. More importantly, however, the election of Abraham Lincoln to the presidency was twenty-three days in the past. Though Palmer had been an advocate of slavery for many years, it was "the election of Lincoln to the presidency [that] brought Palmer openly into the secessionist camp." Palmer was not alone in the transformation. Shortly after the same election, another Presbyterian, the Reverend Moses Drury Hoge of Richmond exclaimed: "We regard the election of Lincoln as the greatest calamity that ever befell this Union." Mitchell Snay has written: "The triumph of Abraham Lincoln in the presidential election of 1860 made the fear of a Northern antislavery majority a reality. The victory of the Republican Party—with its undisguised threat to envelope the slave South with a cordon of free states—triggered the final transformation from Southern sectionalism to Southern nationalism."[30]

Palmer began by reminding his congregation "that I have never intermeddled with political questions. . . . I have preferred to move among you as a preacher of righteousness belonging to a kingdom not of this world." However, as preachers throughout the South had recognized, the present crisis was a religious and moral one, which demanded a response by religious and moral leaders. Palmer noted that that "which now places us upon the brink of revolution, was, in its origin, a question of morals and religion. It was debated in ecclesiastical councils before it entered legislative halls." The central issue in the crisis, according to Palmer, was slavery, which was a "trust providentially committed to us." It was, then, the duty of the South "to conserve and to perpetuate the institution of slavery as now existing." The "black race," said Palmer, was ordained to serve. "We know better than others," he declared, "that every attribute of their character fits them for dependence and servitude. By nature, the most affectionate and loyal of all races beneath the sun, they are also the most helpless; and no calamity can befall them greater than the loss of that protection they enjoy under this patriarchal system." Palmer then widened the issue, affirming that in the South, "we defend the cause of God and religion. The Abolition spirit is undeniably atheistic." The preacher continued:

> To the South the highest position is assigned, of defending, before all nations, the cause of all religion and of all truth. In this trust, we are resisting the power which wars against constitutions, and laws and compacts, against Sabbaths and sanctuaries, against family, the State and the church; which blasphemously invades the prerogatives of God, and rebukes the Most High for the errors of his administration, which, if it cannot snatch the reins of empire from his grasp, will lay the universe in ruins at his feet.

The election of Lincoln had brought the crisis to a head. "The North," said Palmer, "with unexampled unanimity, have cast their ballot for a candidate who is sectional, who represents a party that is sectional, and the ground of that sectionalism, prejudiced against the established and constitutional rights and immunities and institutions of the South." The only recourse left to the South was for the states to call conventions and affirm their intention to secede. "Let the people in all the Southern States," intoned Palmer, "in solemn counsel assembled, reclaim the powers they have delegated. . . . Let them, further, take all the necessary steps looking to separate and independent existence, and initiate measures for forming a new and homogeneous confederacy."[31]

By the early nineteenth century, the southern preachers were nearly unanimous in their defense and support of slavery. Loveland has observed that "in the early nineteenth century, preachers who opposed slavery either left the South or fell silent." Loveland continues by noting that as early as "the 1820s there were virtually no ministers in the South who might have provided an antislavery example to the younger generation of evangelicals."[32] As will be demonstrated later, the proslavery stance was never unanimous among the southern clergy, but it was nearly so. Southern society and culture exerted all kinds of pressures to stifle dissenting voices.

Most preachers were anxious to prove their southern loyalties, for there was a certain suspicion among some in the South that the clergy could not really be trusted on the slavery issue. Many recalled the opposition of evangelical leaders to slavery in the eighteenth century. Others had noticed the close association of abolitionists with religion and wondered if a sharp distinction could really be drawn between southern clergy and northern clergy. Many of these clerics had attended the same schools and, at one time, commingled in the same ecclesiastical circles. Perhaps most damaging of all, when the American Antislavery Society in 1835 sent thousands of pamphlets and other materials into the South denouncing slavery, it was duly noted that many of these inflammatory pieces were sent to southern clergy. The southern preachers were well aware of the finger of suspicion that some were pointing in their direction. In September 1835, a Baptist association in Virginia complained: "We regret that in consequence of having certain incendiary publications addressed to us, without our knowledge or consent, our ministry should be censured and suspected in some degree as aiding and abetting the Northern fanatics in their nefarious designs." The following month a Baptist newspaper in Charleston nervously exclaimed: "We know not who can be safe, when even the open advocates of slavery are denounced as abolitionists." Because of such suspicions, many clergy felt a great need to prove their southern loyalties. Carl N. Degler has written of this period that "it must not be forgotten that antislavery sentiment was dangerous." Snay has recorded three incidents in 1835 where suspicion of clergymen produced intimidation.

In Benton, Alabama, the Rev. James A. Butler was found in possession of a religious journal that contained an article on emancipation. Butler was summoned before Benton's Committee of Vigilance and Safety, where he convinced more than 200 citizens that he opposed abolitionists. His integrity having been questioned by an anonymous writer to the Charleston *Mercury*, Aaron G. Brewer, pastor of the Methodist Protestant Church of Charleston, felt obliged to offer proof of his advocacy of "Southern Institutions." In Laurensville, Georgia, the Rev. John S. Wilson was suspected of antislavery connections. Three clergymen, each representing one of the major denominations, had to testify at a public meeting that Wilson "had uniformly and at all times when conversing upon the subject, censured and disapproved of the conduct of the Abolitionists." Only after this testimony was Wilson safe.[33]

As the slavery issue eventually culminated in calls for secession, by early 1861, the voices of the southern preachers were nearly unanimous in their support of a separate southern Confederacy. Once again, the pressures to bring about this conformity were prodigious. Richard E. Beringer and his colleagues have written that "Southern clergymen who expressed pro-Union sentiment, as a few did, were usually removed from the pulpit by the congregation or perhaps even expelled from church membership."[34] Many of the southern clergy were much slower in coming to an acceptance of secession than they had been in giving their support to slavery. Several had to be converted by time, circumstances, and political/social forces. Two prominent and influential southern clerics who experienced this tortuous conversion from pro-Union to anti-Union sentiments were Robert Lewis Dabney, Presbyterian from Virginia, and his fellow Presbyterian from South Carolina, James Henley Thornwell.

Dabney held Union loyalties and vigorously opposed secession as late as early 1861. On November 1, 1860, he delivered a sermon in the College Church of Hampton Sidney, Virginia, entitled, "The Christian's Best Motive For

Patriotism." In the sermon, Dabney argued that the Church had a responsibility to save the nation from the destruction of a civil war. If the Church fails to do this, he announced, "its guilt will be second only to that of the apostate Church which betrayed the Savior of the world." Blaming the crisis upon "reckless and incapable" politicians, Dabney urged his listeners to heed "the law of God rather than the unrighteous behests of party." After South Carolina seceded from the Union, Dabney referred to that state as "the little impudent vixen" and accused her of being "as great a pest as the Abolitionists." In January 1861, he appealed once more to Christians, urging them to remain loyal to the Union. Lincoln's election, he argued, was not a reason for secession, "which could never be right under any circumstances." Three months later, however, after Lincoln called for troops in response to the surrender of Fort Sumter, Dabney's southern sentiments superseded his Union loyalties, and he became a proponent of secession and a southern Confederacy. He enlisted as a chaplain in the Confederate army where he served on the staff of Stonewall Jackson.[35]

James Henley Thornwell was another example of a latecomer to the secessionist ranks. In 1850, Thornwell passionately opposed the idea of secession. Writing to a friend, he declared, "the prospect of disunion is one which I cannot contemplate without absolute horror. . . . I have hardly been able to sleep in consequence of my deep conviction with which I am oppressed of the evils that threaten us." Early the following year, he wrote an article in the *Southern Presbyterian Review* that was severely critical of South Carolina's bent toward disunion. "Single-handed secession," he declared, "however it might be justified in a crisis in which the Federal Government had become openly pledged to the extinction of slavery, under the present circumstances of our country is recommended by not a single consideration that we are able to discover, of wisdom, patriotism or honour."[36]

Ten years later, Thornwell changed his mind. On

November 21, 1860, two weeks after Lincoln's election, in a sermon at the First Presbyterian Church of Columbia, he called for secession and reminded that "even though our cause be just, and our course approved of Heaven, our path to victory may be through a baptism of blood. Liberty has her martyrs and confessors as well as religion." In late December of that same year, a few days after South Carolina had become the first state to pass an ordinance of secession, Thornwell wrote in a letter: "I believe that we have done right. I do not see any course that was left to us. I am heart and hand with the State in her move." He then wrote an article in which he tried "to influence public opinion in states which have not seceded" and declared, "A free people can never consent to their own degradation." He held out the hope that the division could take place and two nations could be formed "without a jostle or a jar." Anne C. Loveland has commented that Thornwell's transformation on secession was "representative of the majority of southern evangelicals. Although opposed to disunion in the 1850s, they supported secession in 1860–1861."[37]

James M. McPherson has described the degree of southern hostility toward the North in the first months of 1860.

> Every Yankee in the South became *persona non grata*. Some of them received a coat of tar and feathers and a ride out of town on a rail. A few were lynched. The citizens of Boggy Swamp, South Carolina, ran two northern tutors out of the district. "Nothing definite is known of their abolitionist sentiments," commented a local newspaper, "but being from the North, and, therefore, necessarily imbued with doctrines hostile to our institutions, their presence in this section has become obnoxious." The northern- born president of an Alabama college had to flee for his life. . . . Thirty-two representatives in the South of New York and Boston firms arrived in Washington reporting "indignation so great against Northerners that they were compelled to return and abandon their business.[38]

By the time the war began in April 1861, the southern clergy were nearly unanimous in their support of slavery and secession. From 1830 to 1861, a deliberate and concerted effort took place in the South to achieve and enforce this nearly unanimous perspective. During these years, a winnowing process happened, whereby a conscious attempt was made to separate the chaff from the wheat in order to "cleanse" the South from nonconformist views. The effort was largely successful, but never completely so. In spite of great economic, social, political, and even physical pressures, there always remained a few members of the clergy who continued to oppose slavery, and later secession. In spite of frightening intimidations, even threats against life itself, there were a few ministers who would not succumb to the winnowing process. Chapter 2 is the story of some of these southern clerics who defied the tide of public opinion and social forces and the consequences they paid for their defiance.

During the winnowing years, the pressures exerted on the southern clergy to conform were not just over social and political issues but also on matters that were specifically religious in nature. Though religious liberalism and heterodoxy had once been tolerated in the South, after 1830, the South began to display a marked repugnance toward deviations from orthodoxy. Clement Eaton has written that "the two great taboos in the social life of the Old South were the criticism of Southern slavery and heterodoxy in religion." As has been noted, the two taboos were closely related in the minds of many Southerners. "The growing need of defending the institution of slavery . . . tended to produce religious uniformity in the South. Only by a narrow and literal interpretation of the Scriptures could slavery be given the high moral sanction of the church."

Between the death of Jefferson on July 4, 1826 and the last prophetic speech of Calhoun, March 4, 1850, a great change took place in the Southern states. The liberal ideas of the eighteenth century were in large part discarded. . . . The eighteenth century cosmopoliticism of the Tidewater gave way to an intensely local point of view. . . . The profound orthodoxy of the South in 1860 was revealed by the virtual absence of liberal sects below the Potomac. . . . Although the majority of the Northern people would have sympathized with the devotion of the South to orthodoxy, the difference between the two sections was that the Northern states nourished an important minority of skeptics and religious liberals.[39]

Once the war began in the spring of 1861, the pressures to conform became even more intense, for then nonconformity could be equated with treason. Strong denunciations were heaped upon those who sowed doubt about, destroyed confidence in, and were in any way disloyal to the Confederacy. The Baptists in Elon, Virginia, recorded their thoughts about those who failed to carry out their responsibilities: "The man who is not willing to work for the freedom which God has given us, is a traitor to his country, a hypocrite in the church and unfit to die."[40] Many sermons thundered words of judgment upon any who would question the objectives and pronouncements of the Confederacy. Thomas Dunaway's 1864 sermon was representative.

Whoever deals in inflammatory speeches, or heavy complaints, is not the friend but the enemy of his country. Whoever seeks to bring our rulers, civil or military, into disrepute, and thus lessens the confidence of the people in the government of their choice, or in any manner sows the seed of discontent, is working against the peace and welfare of the country.[41]

Such judgments had a direct impact upon the war's duration. In warfare, the preachers proclaimed, it was not the number of soldiers nor the competency of generals that determined the tide of battle; it was God who brought victory, and it was God who administered defeat. Therefore, no matter how bleak a present situation might be, or how disastrous the latest defeat suffered on the battlefield, there was always hope. God could change everything, suddenly and dramatically, if he so desired. So the bloodshed and killing continued in the Civil War long after defeat seemed obvious; for God was the God of history, the God who still worked miracles upon the world's stage, the God who brought forth the impossible, the God who could easily turn heartbreaking defeat into glorious victory. Therefore, when the dark shadows began to fall upon the Confederacy, the clergy were still there, still inspiring, and still holding out hope. Thus, Benjamin Morgan Palmer, in December 1863, five months after Vicksburg and Gettysburg, before the General Assembly of South Carolina, attempted to rekindle the flickering flame. "The language of true prayer," he exclaimed, "is never the cry of supine imbecility, nor the wail of craven despondency. It is always the language of hope and expectation. . . . I thank God that, in the darkest hour, I have never despaired of the republic." It was the ministers who inspired the South to keep on fighting, to continue the shedding of blood, to perpetuate the carnage, when the cause was obviously lost. Beringer writes: "Religion played a greater role in the Confederate experience than in that of the Union because the South needed it more, for as military power ebbed away, the will of the people needed more and more reinforcement if the Confederacy was to survive. In a time of defeat, piety could do what military victories did in better times."[42]

Historian Drew Gilpin Faust, in *The Creation of Confederate Nationalism*, has offered some summary statements as to the contribution of the Christian religion to a Confederate nationalism.

> The most fundamental source of legitimacy for the Confederacy was Christianity. Religion provided a transcendent framework for southern nationalism. . . . Nationhood had to be tied to higher ends. The South, it

seemed, could not just be politically independent; it wanted to believe it was divinely chosen. . . . The analogy between the Confederacy and the chosen Hebrew nation was invoked so often as to be transformed into a figure of everyday speech. Like the United States before it, the Confederacy became the redeemer nation, the new Israel[43]

By 1864, it had become obvious to most observers that a Confederate defeat was inevitable. Peace organizations and movements were springing up all over the South. Large numbers of soldiers were deserting the Confederate army. Many of the preachers in the South, however, were not ready to give up the fight. They urged the people to continue the struggle and labeled as traitors those who pursued peace. On February 28, 1864, John Paris, a Methodist chaplain in the Confederate army, delivered a powerful sermon, which was widely distributed, upon the deaths of twenty-two Confederate soldiers who had been executed by hanging for the crime of desertion. Paris had visited each of the condemned men in their cells before they went to their deaths. He remarked that these men had been good and honest individuals but had become the victims of mischievous home influences. These influences were saying: "We are whipt!" "We might as well give up!" "It is useless to fight any longer!" These misguided, even evil, voices were urging peace, Paris asserted. The deserting soldiers, according to Paris, had received the punishment they deserved, but the real culprits were civilians who had spread their "poisonous contagion of treason" to the troops. Paris singled out the pulpit and the press for special condemnation. "When they [pulpit and press] see [their] Government engaged in a bloody struggle for existence, and show themselves opposed to its efforts to maintain its authority by all constitutional and legal means, such a press, and such pulpits should receive no support for an hour from a people that would be free. The seal of condemnation should consign them to oblivion." Paris warned of the terrors that would befall the South if the North should triumph. Rather than succumb or submit, Paris urged his listeners "to fight it out to the bitter end."[44]

In spite of threats and warnings throughout the years of the Civil War, a few clergy members could still be found throughout the South during this time who would not submit to the regional point of view. A very few continued to renounce slavery. A larger number, though upholding slavery, would not support secession. The idea of breaking away from the Union, especially at the cost of a bloody war, was abhorrent and unacceptable. What happened to these nonconformists, these dissenters, these traitors, from 1861 to 1865 is the topic of chapter 3.

Two

The Winnowing Years, 1830–1861

RICHARD FULLER, a Baptist clergyman who was born and raised in South Carolina, received a degree from Harvard in 1824. Eight years later, he became the pastor of a Baptist church in Beaufort, South Carolina, a position he would hold for fifteen years. In 1844, he and the Reverend Francis Wayland, president of Brown University, became involved in a debate over slavery through an exchange of letters. Wayland opposed slavery; Fuller defended it. The argument, carried out with great skill and respect on the part of both participants, was in 1845 published in a book, *Domestic Slavery Considered as a Scriptural Institution.* Fuller, using political, historical, and biblical arguments, defended the institution of slavery, urging that the abuses of the institution not be confused with the institution itself. Countering Wayland's thesis that slavery was a sin, Fuller replied that "what God sanctioned in the Old Testament, and permitted in the New, cannot be sin." He pointed out the many examples and teachings recorded in the Old Testament whereby slavery is a way of life ordained by God. "The New Testament," affirmed Fuller, "is not silent as to slavery; it recognizes the relation, and commands slaves to obey their masters." Relating the teachings of the Gospel to contemporary times, Fuller continued: "Jesus and his apostles found slavery existing as a part of the social organization. Should they appear now, they would find the same institution here. They did not declare it to be a sin, but by precept and example permitted it to continue; making it, however, a relation not of oppression and crime, but of justice and love."[1]

Fuller was a leader in the formation of the Southern Baptist Convention in 1845, served two years as its president, and preached its first annual sermon in 1846. In 1847, Fuller moved to Baltimore where he became the pastor of the Seventh Baptist Church until 1871. He then became the minister of Eutaw Baptist Church in the same city until his death in 1876. His reason for moving to Baltimore from South Carolina was that Baltimore was located in a border state where he could more closely observe what was happening on both sides of the ever-deepening and threatening sectional crisis.

On January 21, 1851, Fuller delivered an address before the American Colonization Society in which he was critical of both abolitionism and southern extremism. He suggested that the South was overly sensitive on the subject of slavery and should allow open debate on the issue. He urged the North to make concessions and for the South to do the same. The South must realize, exclaimed Fuller, that slavery "fosters indolence and luxury." Seeming to contradict his 1844 position, Fuller asserted that "slavery is not a good thing, and a thing to be perpetuated." He offered colonization as a "middle ground." Congress should grant money for the purchase of slaves from masters and then pay the passage of these former slaves to Liberia.[2] The previously popular and influential Fuller stirred up great hostility and resentment toward himself throughout the South because of his "middle ground" speech. In spite of efforts to explain and tone down his remarks, Fuller never regained his previous stature in the South. The reaction to Fuller's address was an example of the South's unwillingness to hear, much less tolerate, a different point of view, "middle ground" though it was.

Fuller's fellow Baptist from South Carolina, William Henry Brisbane, suffered even greater consequences for his challenge to prevailing sentiments. Unlike Fuller, Brisbane attempted to remain in South Carolina where he took an earlier and stronger stance in opposition to slavery than did Fuller. It is of interest to note the development of Brisbane's thought in regards to slavery. In 1834, he wrote an article for the *Charleston Mercury*, "Has Man a Right to Hold Property in Man?" Some think the essay was an attempt to assuage his own conscience for holding slaves. He found in the Bible the justification for which he was looking and wrote "that man's mind must be awfully perverted by prejudice, who does not see it." Brisbane reprinted the article on April 17, 1835, in the *Southern Baptist and General Intelligencer* of which he was editor. In that same year he used his paper to taunt the abolitionists, declaring that immediate emancipation would be ruinous to both the South and the slaves themselves.

In early July 1835, Brisbane issued a challenge to those in the North whereby he solicited anyone to come forth and show him any biblical teaching that forbade slaveholding. "When it comes," he declared, "we will bow with submission to God, and twenty-eight slaves shall be immediately emancipated." On July 8, Brisbane read an article by the aforementioned Francis Wayland, the articulate antislavery president of Brown University. Brisbane found Wayland's antislavery argument to be compelling. In his diary, he confided that Wayland's biblical arguments against slavery were unanswerable and he would uphold his public promise to free his slaves.

For the next five years, Brisbane held to a position whereby he opposed both slavery and the abolitionists. In an article during this period, he declared his conviction—a conviction that seemed to be at variance with the facts—that most Southerners would willingly free their slaves if they could be compensated at "half the value of their slaves." At the same time, he urged Northerners to censure the abolitionists, "to arrest these misguided fanatics and consign them and their works to the contempt and shame and obscurity which they deserve." In private and in public, the antislavery Brisbane emphasized, "I am no Abolitionist."

Such a stance created problems for the Baptist minister. Though a few supported him for his views, most, especially family and friends, thought him seriously impaired in judgment. Though never threatened, Brisbane was snubbed and scorned by previous friends and acquaintances. Several months after his conversion to an antislavery position, Brisbane had not yet freed his slaves. In April 1836, due to financial problems, Brisbane was forced to sell five of his slaves for $2,000. In the same month, he resigned his editorship of the *Southern Baptist and General Intelligencer.* Financial reversals continued to mount, and in January 1838, Brisbane sold the remainder of his property, which included both land and slaves, keeping one slave family "to wait upon us." In February, the Brisbanes moved to Cincinnati.

The move did not improve Brisbane's financial status. In January 1840, close to financial destitution, Brisbane became an abolitionist and sought to earn money for speeches given in behalf of the cause. This former South Carolina clergyman had changed his stance once again. Now, he was both antislavery and pro-abolitionist. When financial conditions slightly improved, Brisbane, in December 1841, bought back and emancipated all but three of his former slaves. Brisbane's story was the story of other antislavery clergy in the South. That region had become a place where one could not comfortably live. Either a person with antislavery convictions had to be quiet about his convictions or he had to move to the North. Brisbane, along with many others, chose to move.[3]

Some clergy who moved did not do so voluntarily. In August 1859, two ministers of the Methodist Episcopal Church, Solomon McKinney and "Parson" Blount were driven from Dallas by citizens of the city. McKinney was administered seventy lashes before his expulsion. McKinney's and Blount's expulsions had their roots in the schism of the Methodist Church in 1844 and the formation of the Methodist Episcopal Church, South, as a proslavery, states' rights denomination. Several Texas Methodists, especially in north Texas, for varying reasons chose to remain with the original body. Therefore, the original organization continued to maintain churches in Texas and furnished ministers to pastor those churches. Some of those churches, in the years just before the Civil War, were fairly successful and actually increased their memberships. The majority of Texans, however, viewed those "Northern Methodists" with great suspicion and hostility. Regardless of what sentiments a particular minister held, because he was a part of that northern group, it was automatically assumed that the minister was an abolitionist and was guilty of promoting slave insurrections. This was the kind of situation in which McKinney and Blount found themselves. McKinney protested his innocence, claiming that he had come to Texas on his own, had received no salary from outside sources for his ministry, and was not guilty of anti-slavery actions. The editor of the *Texas Christian Advocate* (Galveston), one of the official regional weeklies of the Methodist Episcopal Church, South, wrote over a year after the incident that he was sure McKinney had lied "because . . . it is easier to believe that men will lie . . . than that they will act so very much worse as he charges them with doing."[4]

A more serious consequence was administered to another "Northern Methodist" minister, Anthony Bewley, who, during the night of September 13, 1860, was hanged by a Fort Worth vigilance committee that charged him with plotting a slave insurrection in Texas. Bewley was no Yankee who had come south to cause trouble but a native of Tennessee whose ministry had been practiced in the slave states of Missouri, Arkansas, and Texas. His southern origins, however, failed to save him and may have only increased the hostility against him. It was easy to perceive him as a traitor who should have known better. The fifty-six-year-old Bewley had been assigned to the Fort Worth area by the Methodist Episcopal Church just at that time when fears of a slave insurrection were at their height in the state. Texans in general, and vigilante committees in particular, were anxiously looking for dangerous and suspicious characters. Though Bewley was a moderate in his views on slavery who measured his words very carefully so as not to arouse unwanted hostility, public wrath began to turn on him. He had come to Texas at the wrong time, and under the auspices of the Methodist Episcopal Church, believed by many in Texas to be dedicated to the destruction of the southern way of life.

In July 1860, Bewley, sensing his personal danger, fled from Fort Worth with his wife and youngest child. They went first to Indian Territory where they united with other members of the family. Then they proceeded to Caseville, Missouri. In the meantime, vigilance committees in the Fort Worth area offered a $1,000 reward for Bewley's arrest. A posse was formed that tracked Bewley to Missouri, captured him, and, with their victim, began the journey back to Fort Worth. They arrived in Fayetteville, Arkansas, on September 4, where Bewley would have been hung if not for the intervention of the county sheriff. On the evening of September 13, Bewley and his captors arrived in Fort Worth. Sometime after the evening meal—no one seems to know what specific time—Bewley was hanged at a site known as Crawford's limb, a tree from which another accused abolitionist had recently been lynched. The evidence against Bewley, who was never given the benefit of trial, was scant. His murder brought the activities of the Methodist Episcopal Church to an end in Texas until after the Civil War.[5] In a letter to his wife and children, written while he was being held captive in Fayetteville, Bewley proclaimed his innocence and said farewell.

> Fayetteville, Ark.
> September 5, 1860
> Dear Wife and Children,
>   I never took up my pen under such circumstances before. After I left there that day, I was hurried on, and the next day, about nine or ten o'clock, we got to Fayetteville. I am here yet. . . .

At night I am chained fast to some person, and in the day I have liberty to walk about with the guard. I have been in general tolerable; though my company in general has not been as desirable as some. They are now after Tom Willet. As soon as they succeed in getting him, I suppose they will set out with us to Texas . . . hand us over to the Fort Worth Committee, and receive the reward. Then we will, I suppose, be under their supervision to do with us as seemeth them good. And if this takes place, dear and much beloved wife and loving children, I shall never in this life expect to see you. . . . The reason why I speak so, in these times of heated excitement, mole-hills are raised mountain-high, and when there are none, it is frequently imagined they see something. That being the case, it seems enough to know that we are "North Methodists," as they are called; and from what we learned in Texas about that Fort Worth Committee, they had sworn vengeance against all such folks. I expect when they get us we will go the trip. But, dear wife and children . . . know that so far as I am concerned, all these things are false. You have been with me, and you know as well as I do that none of these things has ever been countenanced about our house. . . . You will have to spend the remaining part of your life as a bereaved widow, with your orphan children, with one blind daughter. . . . As I was taken away, and was not permitted to see you, that I might bid you and the children farewell, I have to do it this way, and would say to all to try to continue your way onward to heaven. . . . I now close by subscribing myself your affectionate husband and father.

Anthony Bewley

You will doubtless preserve this imperfect scroll.

The next day Bewley added a few more lines to his letter.

This is September 6th, 1860

City of Fayetteville, Ark.

I, with a portion of the vigilance committee, will leave Fayetteville to-night sometime. The Committee has returned without Willett, and have given up hunting him any more.

Anthony Bewley[6]

James W. Silver has noted that "Texas vigilantes chased many a Northern Methodist out of the state." James Marten hints at other reasons as to why some Methodist ministers in Texas received such harsh treatment.

Mere chance cannot explain why some dissenters suffered the slings and arrows of vigilantism while others remained to a greater or less degree unmolested. Economic status, social position, and geography all played a part. Hapless Methodist missionaries, for instance, were more vulnerable to expulsion or violence than prominent politicians, attorneys, or planters, who usually had to contend only with angry epithets and editorials.[7]

Marten notes that "vigilant southerners used a wide variety of techniques to suppress heresy, or to convince their friends and colleagues of the errors of their ways." Speaking specifically of the Bewley incident, Marten writes that "the members of the mob who lynched Bewley simply played out the southern ritual of eliminating ideas that posed a threat to a way of life that by 1860 seemed to face enemies from all sides, particularly from the North." After writing of the various "political, rhetorical, and social versions of censorship and punishment," Marten emphasizes that such methods "demonstrated a growing southern defensiveness in the face of the rising power of the North, along with a commitment to protecting slavery and providing for its expansion. These ideas created a sense of loyalty to the South that encouraged southerners to lash out at any external or internal enemy that challenged southern values or interests."[8]

Such lashing out at an "external or internal enemy" was not confined to the lower South. "Censorship and punishment" for the purpose of insuring conformity was also practiced in the upper South and border states. Observe the consequences of the "missionary" efforts by Daniel Worth in North Carolina. Worth was born in 1795 to a Quaker family in Guilford County, North Carolina. Daniel, his mother, father, and other family members moved to Indiana in the spring of 1822 as a part of a larger Quaker migration from North Carolina due to disenchantment over the state's slavery policies. In 1831, Worth became a part of the Methodist Episcopal Church but was soon disillusioned with the denomination because of its failure to take a bold stand against slavery. At that time, the Methodist division, North and South, had not yet taken place, and the organization was attempting to appease slaveholders and nonslaveholders alike. Thus, in 1842, Worth was instrumental in organizing the Wesleyan Methodist Church, a group that had splintered from the larger Methodist body in order to adopt a strong ecclesiastical stance against slavery. Two years later, Worth was ordained by the new denomination. For the next several years, Worth pastored churches, served as president of the General Conference of the Wesleyan Methodist Church, and was involved in various antislavery activities.

In 1857, when he was sixty-two years of age, Worth was sent by the American Missionary Association to, among other things, preach against slavery in North Carolina. As a part of his ministry in North Carolina, Worth distributed numerous copies of Hinton Rowan Helper's book, *The Impending Crisis of the South: How to Meet It*, which was not only a vehement denunciation of slavery but also a scathing attack upon the South and its way of life.[9] Until John Brown's raid on Harper's Ferry in October 1859, Worth continued on with his ministry facing relatively few obstacles. Carl N. Degler, in commenting upon how much Worth was allowed to do, writes that "it was always possible, at least in the upper South, to discuss the disadvantages, if not the outright evil, of slavery, as long as two conditions were met." The first condition was "that the person making the criticism be a native Southerner." Worth was a native North Carolinian and understood its advantage. In a letter to his nephew on April 30, 1858, Worth spoke of personal qualities he thought provided him protection:

> There would seem to be a hand of Providence in it, as I can preach, and have done it, as strong and direct against slavery as you ever heard me in the north, and I believe there is not another man that could. The reasons for this I cannot explain in a short letter, but are mainly my southern birth on the very spot where I preach; my age, which has reached a point to attract somewhat of reverence, and influential connectionship (my cousins are slaveholders and are men of great popularity), my wife's very large relationship, and my general acquaintance with the old men of the country, and with the fathers of the young.[10]

The second condition mentioned by Degler was that criticisms must not be made "in the context of a threat to the slave system" that might be taking place at the time. Such a threat was John Brown's raid in Virginia during the fall of 1859. After that incident at Harper's Ferry, matters changed drastically for Daniel Worth. In late November, the *North Carolina Presbyterian*, a publication that had been denouncing Worth for at least a year, intensified its attacks upon the Wesleyan preacher. Calling Worth a "run-mad fanatic," the paper asserted that "society must be protected against cut-throats and assassins, and the sword of the civil magistrate is the instrument which God had appointed for their punishment." Other religious and secular publications joined the *North Carolina Presbyterian*, asking, "Why is this man not arrested?" One paper suggested that the people take the law into their own hands. On December

22, 1859, Worth was arrested and placed in the jail at Greensboro. Bail was denied because the offense was considered a capital crime. The cell was cold and lacked adequate bedding.[11]

Two days later, on Christmas Eve, Worth was given a preliminary hearing. A newspaper ran the following account of the hearing.

> Some fifteen or sixteen witnesses were examined. It was proved that he had used in his sermons the strongest and vilest incendiary language, and had circulated Helper's book. Among other things he had declared publicly that he had "no respect for the laws of North Carolina" . . . that "they were enacted by adulterers, drunkards, and gamblers" . . . and that he "would not have had old John Brown hung for a thousand worlds."[12]

During the hearing, a package containing two hundred copies of Helper's book came open in the post office at Raleigh. The books had been sent to Worth in care of another person's name and address. Once the courts had been notified as to the contents of this package, there was a "bookburning in the public square." After the hearing, Worth was held over in the Greensboro jail to await trial in the spring.

While in jail, Worth suffered greatly from the cold. Outside temperatures during January 1860 were as low as 2 degrees above zero. One writer has recorded that Worth suffered from frozen feet during that winter. The single benefit from the internment was that it provided protection from a lynch mob. In a letter to his wife, Worth wrote: "I could have given bail, but I sought the security of bolts and prison bars. The fact is, that if I had been outside the prison at Greensboro I would have lost my life through the violence of a mob."[13]

Worth underwent two trials; the first held in Asheboro on March 30, 1860, and the second in Greensboro on April 27. In both trials, Worth was found guilty of disobeying an 1830 North Carolina law that made it illegal to circulate material that could result in a slave uprising. He was sentenced to a year in jail but was spared a whipping, which the law suggested as a penalty for that crime. When Worth appealed his case to the North Carolina Supreme Court, he was temporarily released from jail on making bond. In a moment of freedom, Worth made his way to the safety of the North.[14]

In response to the Nat Turner revolt in Southampton, Virginia, in the late summer of 1831, where about sixty whites, most of them women and children, were brutally slain, the renowned slavery debate of 1832 was conducted in the Virginia legislature. Joseph Clarke Robert has noted that the debate, the "final and most brilliant of the Southern attempts to abolish slavery represents the line of demarcation between a public willing to hear the faults of slavery and one intolerant of criticism." Robert goes on to comment that "Virginia was not without antislavery sentiment in the period from 1832 to 1860, but expressions of this nature were infrequent, cautious, and usually private."[15] There were, however, during these twenty-eight years, a few voices in Virginia still openly critical of slavery, and some of these protesting voices belonged to the clergy.

Soon after the slavery debate in Virginia, the Reverend John Hersey, a Methodist preacher, wrote a book called *Appeal to Christians on the Subject of Slavery*. The book, which included excerpts from the slavery debates, presented a moral argument against slavery. Proclaiming that black men and white men were brothers, Hersey asked: "Would it be esteemed honorable, or merciful, or affectionate in any human being to hold his own brother in bondage for life, and make a slave of him?" Reminding his readers that the Gospel called them to love all their neighbors as themselves, Hersey proclaimed that neighbors included "the Africans, the slaves, the beggars." Calling attention to the Golden Rule—"do unto others as ye would they should do unto you"—Hersey questioned whether anyone would be willing to be another's slave under any circumstances. The slaves must be freed, he contended. However, Hersey pointed out, America was not the place where these freed people should live. Prejudice was too prevalent in America, North and South, and most Americans considered "black skin as a badge of disgrace and inferiority." In America, Hersey sadly commented, the black man would always be "degraded, insulted, and oppressed." Therefore, Hersey proposed colonization to Liberia over a thirty-to-forty-year period, which he estimated would cost $3 million a year. The money could be raised if the two million Christians in the United States would contribute $1.50 per year for colonization. A second edition of Hersey's *Appeal* was published in 1833, and a third edition about ten years later. Although the book was at first tolerated, as the northern abolitionists accusations intensified, the book became increasingly unacceptable. Many copies of the book were burned in Richmond, and Hersey was forced to leave Virginia and move to a northern state.[16]

A Reverend J. D. Paxton was forced to leave his church at Cumberland, Virginia, because he had written an anti-slavery article that was published in a religious paper. After his banishment from the church, Paxton wrote and published a small book, *Letters on Slavery*. He called slavery a moral evil and declared that Christians were morally obligated to work for its destruction. Slavery, Paxton wrote, was a contradiction to the teachings and spirit of the Gospel, and it corrupted the character of slaveowners. He deplored the policy of silence that Virginia and other southern states had imposed on the subject of slavery and predicted that open discussion would lead to the eventual downfall of the institution.[17]

Another clergy voice from Virginia that openly denounced slavery was that of the Reverend Wesley Smith. As a Methodist, Smith deplored the schism of 1844. In a series of lectures during 1855 throughout western Virginia, he defended the Methodist Episcopal Church and declared that it had done the right thing when it voted that a southern bishop, James O. Andrew, could no longer hold office because he owned slaves. Smith furthermore declared that slavery was an evil and the Fugitive Slave Law was unjust. As did J. D. Paxton, Smith urged his state to allow freedom of speech on the subject of slavery. When he spoke at Buckhannon, a mob tried to silence him. Soon after that incident, he published his antislavery lecture as a pamphlet.[18]

Even in those border slave states that never joined the Confederacy, there were earnest attempts to silence criticism of the peculiar institution. In Kentucky, Robert J. Breckinridge's assault on slavery began early and was relentlessly pursued until the end of the war. In 1830, he published a booklet, *Hints on Slavery*, in which he declared that slavery was "an ulcer eating its way into the very heart of the state." He urged gradual emancipation and warned his readers as to what would happen if the slaves were not soon freed. "Men will not always remain slaves," he warned. "No kindness can soothe the spirit of a slave. No ignorance, however abject, can obliterate the indelible stamp of nature, whereby she decreed man free. No cruelty of bondage, however rigorous, can suppress forever the deep yearnings after freedom." Breckinridge had freed his slaves, and his warning came just before the Turner Revolt that so terrified the South. In an 1831 speech, Breckinridge supported colonization as a means to ending slavery. Along with most other proponents of colonization, Breckinridge perceived colonization as a moral answer to ending slavery. The American Colonization Society, he exclaimed, "cherished the hope and the belief also, that the successful prosecution of its objects would offer powerful motives and exert a persuasive influence in favor of emancipation. And it is with this indirect effect of the society that the largest advantage is to result in America."[19]

Breckinridge had served several terms in the Kentucky legislature, but his opposition to slavery and Sunday mails led to political defeat in 1831. He then became a Presbyterian minister, serving churches in Baltimore and Lexington. He was a fierce crusader who waged battles not just against slavery but against Catholics, Universalists, and whiskey drinking. On January 4, 1861—two months after Lincoln's election, two weeks after South Carolina had seceded, and as other states were preparing to follow South Carolina's lead—Breckinridge delivered a discourse in Lexington, Kentucky, entitled, "The Union to Be Preserved." The minister passionately exclaimed "that we should strive with all our might to prevent . . . the annihilation of the nation . . . by tearing it into fragments." Secession was both unconstitutional and immoral. "No state in this Union," asserted Breckinridge, "had any sovereignty at all, independent of, and except as they were 'United States.' . . . The right of secession . . . seems to me . . . to be both immoral and absurd." Slavery, argued Breckinridge, was not relevant to the question of secession. There was no "reason why States with slaves, and States without slaves should not abide together in peace, as portions of the same great nation, as they have done from the beginning." Breckinridge called attention to the absence of debate and dissenting opinion in South Carolina. "We in Kentucky," he asserted, "are tolerant of opinion. Inform yourselves of what is passing of an opposite character throughout South Carolina." In spite of an uncompromising antislavery and antisecession stance, Breckinridge was able to hold prominent positions and responsibilities in Kentucky. "He had the advantage of being the scion of an illustrious Kentucky family" and had received "a splendid education in Northern colleges, including Jefferson, Yale, and Union." Prominent family connections made it possible for him to be superintendent of education in Kentucky from 1847 to 1853 and to go unmolested even during the war years when "he was one of the most violent and influential supporters of the Union cause."[20]

A Kentucky clergyman who lacked prominent family connections and thus suffered more serious consequences for his antislavery words and actions was John Gregg Fee. Born and raised in Kentucky, Fee took undergraduate work in Augusta and Miami colleges before entering Lane Theological Seminary in 1842 to prepare for the ministry. It was at Lane that Fee, the son of slaveholding parents was, after an intense inner struggle, converted to abolitionism. When he informed his parents as to this new direction in his life, he was disinherited by his father. The father denounced the son as disloyal, and warned, "Either you renounce this foolish and traitorous proposal or else you need never darken my door again." The young man had made his choice and was never welcomed back to his family home. Fee committed himself to an antislavery ministry in Kentucky, though much aware of the potential danger in doing so. He founded two antislavery churches in Lewis and Bracken counties, which he served for a number of years. During this time, he was shot at, clubbed, and stoned. He was mobbed twenty-two times, and on two occasions, he was left for dead. Carrying no weapons, he would often pray for and preach to the mobs as they approached him. Though he attempted to prosecute mob leaders in the courts, he met with almost no success in securing convictions. Fee noted in his autobiography, however, that several of these leaders met violent deaths.[21]

In 1853, Fee organized Union Church and a school for children at Berea, Kentucky. Opposed to sectarianism—Fee labeled sects and denominations as "contrary to the spirit of the Gospel, a hindrance to reform"—Union Church was open to all. Eaton has noted that "several Oberlin students came to Berea to teach in the only school in the South where white and black children studied side by side." In 1855, Fee began what would become Berea College, biracial in its student body, modeled after Oberlin College, and financed by funds from the North. In 1859, when Fee was in the Northeast raising money for the college, John Brown's raid occurred. At Henry Ward Beecher's church in Brooklyn, Fee declared: "We want more John Browns, not in manner of action, but in consecration; not to go with carnal weapons but with spiritual."

The Kentucky press misreported Fee's words and claimed that "John G. Fee is in Beecher's church calling for more John Browns." A mob of 750 men met at Richmond, Kentucky, and pledged themselves to ridding their state of Fee and his coworkers. The people in Berea appealed to the governor for protection, but the governor refused the request, and Fee and some of fellow laborers were forced to flee to Cincinnati. In 1863, Fee returned to Kentucky where he worked with black soldiers at Camp Nelson. At war's end, he returned to Berea to once again work in the church and for the college.[22]

Fee's grandson, Edwin Rogers Embree, writes of going with his grandfather in the years after the war to gather subscriptions for his college and school from some of the same men who had persecuted him in earlier days. In Richmond, Kentucky, the grandfather noted: "Son, that man who just gave me a hundred dollars led a mob against me in '54," or, "That man who was telling the race horse story threw me in the Ohio River in '59 and told me if I ever came back to Kentucky he'd kill me with his own hands." Embree remembered that his grandfather "had one big bump on the top of his bald head. An infuriated slaveholder had broken a club there fifty years before. Fortunately, the preacher had just bought a tall stiff hat, and that took most of the blow that had been meant to kill him."[23]

Moncure Daniel Conway discovered that even in the nation's capital the freedom to speak out against slavery was seriously curtailed. Born near Falmouth, Virginia, in 1832 to strict Methodist slaveholding parents, Conway entered the Methodist ministry soon after graduation from Dickinson College in Carlisle, Pennsylvania. While serving two circuits in the Methodist Conference of Maryland, the young Conway became disenchanted with Methodist theology, and at the age of twenty-one, much to the disapproval of his parents, he entered Harvard Divinity School. At Harvard, Conway met Emerson and many of the New England intellectuals of the era. His experiences and education in New England brought focus and direction to changes that had been stirring for some time within the soul of a restless young man. Religiously, Conway became a Unitarian; socially and politically, he became an ardent opponent of slavery.

Conway was called to be the pastor of the Unitarian Church in Washington, where he soon gained the reputation as an outspoken antislavery proponent. In September 1854, he wrote to his father in Falmouth of his intentions to come for a visit. The father replied:

> It is my sincere advice not to come here until there is reason to believe your opinions have undergone material changes on the subject of slavery. If you are willing to expose your own person recklessly, I am not willing to subject myself and family to the hazards of such a visit. Those opinions give me more uneasiness just now than your horrible views on the subject of religion, bad as these last are.[24]

The father indicated that he thought the hostile attitudes of the neighbors were merited. During the following year, Conway disregarded his father's advice and paid a visit to Falmouth. Walking along the streets of the small community, he met a group of young men, some of whom were former schoolmates, who demanded that he leave the community. The men accused him of being an abolitionist and exclaimed, "There is danger in having that kind of man among our servants and you must leave." Conway heeded the instructions and the next day, aboard a steamboat on the Potomac carrying him back to Washington, he wept as he pondered the rejection of his hometown and family.[25]

Though the church that Conway pastored was a liberal one, many in the congregation were uncomfortable with what they perceived as their minister's radical pronouncements on slavery. On Sunday, July 6, 1856, Conway delivered a sermon that he later referred to as "the sermon fatal to my ministry." The sermon's theme was a plea for peace as Conway said, "I saw the approach of civil war." However, much of the discourse was taken up with some of the strongest and most bitter attacks the minister had ever made against slavery.

Of course it would be a waste of breath to appeal to
Slavery for Peace. As well appeal to the fang of the
serpent not to strike as to the poisoned fang of hell. . . .
Is there anything incompatible in buying and selling men
and women made in the image of God on the block and
a violation of the most sacred compacts which sections
can form? . . . Slavery takes naturally to bludgeons or
pistols. . . . For every man in this country Slavery has a
bribe at every pore, and a lash over all who will not obey
its behests. . . . I feel the presence of its great infernal
power in this house to-day,—there lurking among you,
whispering, "Don't stand such preaching as this; if you
do your friends will turn away from you, and you will be
called an abolitionist." It's up here whispering to me, "If
you do not stop this preaching against Slavery, it will
have its cudgel over your head,—your friends will be
fewer even than they are now." Get thee behind me,
cunning Devil![26]

As the service came to its conclusion, Conway recalled
that the members of the congregation "were so troubled
by my discourse that they could not sing. . . . How often
have I remembered the heaviness of that moment." The
following Sunday, a church committee submitted a question to the congregation, "Whether he who thus persists in
this desecration of his pulpit shall continue in the exercise
of his function as pastor, under its authority and with its
sanction?" On October 5, after a heated debate, the Unitarian congregation, by a margin of five votes, dismissed
Conway as the pastor of their church.[27] He immediately
took a pastorate in Cincinnati and, later, a pastorate in Lon-
don, England; he would go on to edit an antislavery newspaper in Massachusetts and eventually would become critical
of Abraham Lincoln's stance on slavery as well as the
president's conduct of the war.

By the spring of 1861 when eleven states had seceded
and the war had commenced, the winnowing process of
the past thirty years had effectively done its work in the
South. Those who criticized and dissented from the stance

of the dominant southern culture and society had to a large degree been weeded out. Nonconforming voices were few in number and difficult to hear. Richard Fuller, William Brisbane, Solomon McKinney, "Parson" Blount, Daniel Worth, John Hersey, John Gregg Fee, and Moncure Conway had all left the South, some forced out and others leaving "voluntarily." These men were representative of many others who could no longer live on their native soil. No one will ever know or be able to estimate the larger number of clerics who shared antislavery sentiments but chose, out of a need to protect themselves, their families, and their vocations, to be silent on the subject. As Anthony Bewley sadly discovered, to even be suspected of dissent on the slavery issue was an extremely dangerous position to hold in many parts of the South.

Yet, after the war began, clergy dissenters could still be found in the South. New issues over which to dissent had been introduced. There were ministers who continued to defend slavery but, after 1861, could not support secession and/or war. As will be recorded in the next chapter, opposition to secession was also dangerous ground, perhaps even more so than opposition to slavery; for to oppose secession and the war were acts of disloyalty, seditious and traitorous positions that were deserving of imprisonment and even death.

Richard Fuller, a Baptist minister, changed his proslavery views after moving from South Carolina to Maryland. Courtesy of Southern Baptist Historical Library and Archives, Nashville, Tennessee.

John Gregg Fee, the founder of Berea College in Kentucky, was
denounced by his family and forced to leave the state because of his
abolitionist views. Courtesy of Berea College.

Moncure Daniel Conway, a Unitarian minister from Washington, D.C., was dismissed from his church because of his antislavery sermons. Photo taken from *Autobiography of Moncure Daniel Conway* (1904).

William G. Brownlow, a Methodist cleric and newspaper publisher in Tennessee, opposed secession and the Civil War, was imprisoned, and eventually forced to leave the state. He later became the governor of Tennessee. Photo taken from *Sketches of the Rise, Progress, and Decline of Secession* by Brownlow (1862).

Charles Gillette, an Episcopal rector in Austin, Texas, opposed his bishop on sectional issues and was dismissed from his church. Photo taken from *The History and Treasures of St. David's Church* by Daisy Barrett Tanner. Courtesy of the parishioners of St. David's Episcopal Church, Austin, Texas.

Melinda Rankin, a Presbyterian missionary worker in Brownsville, Texas, was dismissed from her teaching responsibilities because of alleged northern sympathies. Courtesy of the Presbyterian Historical Society, Philadelphia.

John H. Aughey, a Presbyterian evangelist from Mississippi, was imprisoned and sentenced to death for his opposition to secession. Courtesy of the Presbyterian Historical Society, Philadelphia.

James A. Lyon, the pastor of the First Presbyterian Church in
Columbus, Mississippi, maintained his position in the church though
he strongly and openly opposed secession and the war. Courtesy of
the Presbyterian Historical Society, Philadelphia.

Three

The War Years, 1861–1865

ON DECEMBER 20, 1860, South Carolina became the first state ever to withdraw from the United States of America. The following month, five more states—Mississippi, Florida, Alabama, Georgia, and Louisiana—joined with the Palmetto State in acts of secession. On February 1, 1861, Texas became the seventh state to secede. A week later, representatives from the seven states met in Montgomery, Alabama, to form the Confederacy, a new nation composed of southern states. In mid-April, Fort Sumter was bombarded from the Charleston shoreline and soon surrendered. Lincoln issued his call for troops and the war was on. During April and May, four more states—Virginia, Arkansas, Tennessee, and North Carolina—would secede and join the Confederacy. Departure from the Union, it was proclaimed, was necessary for the preservation of slavery, a divinely ordained and biblically sanctioned way of ordering life. All Christians, all denominations, all churches, and all clergy were called upon to support the new nation with unwavering and unquestioning loyalty. A failure to do so was an act of treason and the consequences for such a crime could be serious. The Confederate army, southern courts, and, most frightening of all, vigilante groups, were diligent in the suppression of dissent. Nevertheless, dissension remained, and some members of the clergy were to be found among the dissenters. There were those who dearly loved their native South but believed that secession and war were not at all in the South's best interest, that such reckless acts would have disastrous consequences. Trying to save the South from what they perceived as suicidal policies and actions, these clerics placed themselves in harm's way.

As would be expected, dissent in the upper South was more prevalent than in the lower or deep South. Bishop James Andrew noted that in the Holston Conference of the Methodist Episcopal Church, South—a conference that included eastern Tennessee and southwestern Virginia— there was a serious division of sentiment among the clergy. Seven ministers belonging to this conference were expelled during the war years for their Unionism. Robert Topp, a distinguished citizen from Memphis, in a letter to Jefferson Davis, wrote of "an old man named Duggan [from east Tennessee], a Methodist preacher [who] was arrested; carried fifty miles on foot (he being a large, fleshly man), refused the privilege of riding his horse, and all they had against him was that, in February last, he had prayed for the Union." The Presbyterians in Tennessee also had their problems in maintaining loyalty to the Confederacy. Several ministers were deposed by a presbytery of the Cumberland Presbyterian Church for Unionism. The Reverend J. S. Hayes, for example, pastor of the Second Presbyterian Church in Nashville, was forced by his congregation in June 1861 to resign from his church because he had refused to pray for the success of the armies of Tennessee and had ignored President Davis's order to observe June 13 as a day of fasting and prayer.[1]

James Madison Pendleton, a Baptist minister and educator in Kentucky and Tennessee, was opposed to slavery and thought the preservation of the Union to be of paramount importance. In his *Reminiscences*, Pendleton recalled: "I deny that the right of revolution can exist under a Republican form of government. . . . Believing that the Confederacy . . . has no right to exist, I had no sympathy with it, and heartily wished its overthrow by the Army and Navy of the United States." Pendleton had pastored a Baptist church in Bowling Green, Kentucky for twenty-four years and, in 1857, became professor of theology at Union University in Murfreesboro, Tennessee, where he lived when the war began. It was of Murfreesboro that Pendleton wrote: "I was known to be a Union man, and it was no advantage to me that nearly all my family connections by blood and marriage, were on the other side." The pastor-professor noted the dangers he faced: "It is said that a certain citizen offered to lead any company that would undertake to hang me." In 1862, Pendleton was forced to leave Tennessee and, for the next three years, served as a pastor in Hamilton, Ohio. In 1865, he began a pastorate in Upland, Pennsylvania, where he would play a major role in the founding of Crozer Theological Seminary.[2]

The most-noted Tennessee clergyman who would not support secession, and thus, the Confederacy, was, of course, William G. "Parson" Brownlow. Born in Virginia, Brownlow moved with his family to Virginia when he was very young. He entered the Methodist ministry in 1826 when he was twenty-one years of age and, for the next ten years, labored as an itinerant preacher. His interest in politics led him into journalism, and in 1849 he became the editor of the *Knoxville Whig*. Under his leadership, the paper came to have the largest circulation of any political paper in the state.

Brownlow, an imposing man, six feet in height, weighing 175 pounds, and the possessor of a powerful voice, seemed to be attracted to controversy. A great believer in the Methodist Church, he fiercely denounced other denominations. In 1834, he wrote a book, *Helps to the Study of Presbyterianism; or An Unsophisticated Exposition of Calvinism*, which was both amusing and greatly critical of the Presbyterians. His heaviest religious attacks, however, were reserved for the Baptist preacher, J. R. Graves, who had written a work entitled *The Great Iron Wheel*. In 1856, "Parson" Brownlow wrote another book, *The Great Iron Wheel Exposed; or Its False Spokes Extracted*, which specifically attacked Graves's work and the Baptists in general. He challenged the Baptists for their beliefs in closed communion and baptism by immersion. He pointed out that while Methodists and most other denominations baptize their converts face foremost, "our Baptist brethren are almost alone in their vulgarity in backing into the church of God."[3]

The "Parson" was also a great defender of slavery. In sermons and editorials, Brownlow was a determined proponent of the "peculiar institution." He challenged any Northerner, providing he was not an African American, to debate with him on the question of slavery. In 1858, an abolitionist named Pryne accepted the challenge, and a well-publicized series of debates took place in Philadelphia. In the debates, Brownlow based his defense of slavery upon a literal interpretation of the Bible. "Abraham," he declared, owned "more slaves than any cotton planter in South Carolina, Georgia, Alabama, or Mississippi; or any tobacco or sugar planter in Virginia or Louisiana." Like many others in the South, Brownlow claimed that slavery had Christianized and civilized the "brutal negroes" from Africa. Slavery, insisted Brownlow, "has brought five times more negroes into the fold of the Church than all the missionary operations in the world combined. Slavery has tamed, civilized, Christianized, if you please, the brutal negroes brought to our shores, by New England kidnappers." Brownlow looked upon the abolitionists as "an unmitigated generation of hypocrites! They stole and sold into perpetual bondage, a race of human beings it was not profitable to keep, and for whom they now, like so many graceless pirates, refuse all warranty." During the debates, Brownlow extolled the South.

> Yes, gentlemen, ours is the land of chivalry, the land of muse, the abode of statesmen, the home of oratory, the dwelling-place of the historian, and of the hero; the scenes of classic recollections and of hallowed associations lie south of Mason and Dixon's Line; and when the South is prostrated (which God in his mercy never intends), the genius of the world will weep amid the ruins of the only true Republic ever known to civilized man![4]

On August 9, 1857, at Temperance Hall in Knoxville, Brownlow delivered "A Sermon on Slavery; A Vindication of the Methodist Church, South," in which he defended the right of Methodists in the South to secede from the national body and form their own separate denomination. Methodists in the North, according to Brownlow, had unjustly attacked the integrity of slaveowners, denying to them what God had given. Interestingly, though Brownlow could defend secession in the Church, he could not tolerate it for the nation. As early as 1832, Brownlow was predicting that the day would soon come when slavery, not the tariff, would be the issue that would shake the government to its very foundations. When that day came, Brownlow promised, in spite of his uncompromising belief in slavery, he would stand by the federal government. As firmly as he had declared for slavery, with equal firmness, he declared for the Union and against secession. In the presidential election of 1860, though Lincoln was not Brownlow's choice, when it looked as though the man from Illinois might be elected, the Parson affirmed: "I will sustain Lincoln if he will go to work to put down the great Southern mob that leads off in such a rebellion." In a speech before the Bell and Everett Club at Knoxville in October 1860, Brownlow asserted:

> These are my sentiments, and these are my purposes; and I am no Abolitionist, but a Southern man. I expect to stand by this Union, and battle to sustain it, though Whiggery and Democracy, Slavery and Abolitionism, Southern rights and Northern wrongs, are all blown to the devil! I will never join in the outcry against the American Union in order to build up a corrupt Democratic party in the South, and to create offices in a new Government for an unprincipled pack of broken-down politicians, who have justly rendered themselves odious by stealing the public money. I may stand alone in the South; but I believe thousands and tens of thousands will stand by me, and, if need be, perish with me in the same cause.[5]

It was because Brownlow so ardently favored slavery that he so vigorously wanted the Union to be preserved. His biographer has written that "Brownlow, who was just as anxious as the most loyal Confederate soldier to preserve slavery, thought that the institution could best be maintained by remaining in the Union and fighting for the rights that amply guaranteed it and protected it under the Federal Constitution." He placed much of the blame for the secession movement upon the churches and their clergy. "The South is now full of these reverend traitors," he charged, "and every branch of the Christian Church is cursed with their labors." In 1862 he declared: "Here, as in all parts of the South, the worst class of men are preachers. They have done more to bring about the deplorable state of things existing in the country than any other class of men." Looking at his own denomination, Brownlow asserted that "at the head of these [denominations] for mischief are the Southern Methodists." His house was the last in Knoxville to display the Union flag, and his newspaper, the Whig, was the last Union newspaper in the South until it was suppressed on October 24, 1861.[6]

On December 6, 1861, Brownlow was arrested and placed in the jail at Knoxville on charges of treason because of his editorials and the suspicion that he may have been involved in the burning of railway bridges the previous week. The latter charge was spurious. Though his imprisonment was brief, Brownlow found it a difficult experience. While there, he suffered from typhoid. E. Merton Coulter has written of Brownlow's confinement.

> The jail was crowded with about 150 Unionists . . . so crowded that some of the prisoners were forced to stand to permit others space on the floor where they might sleep. . . . He found the food very bad. . . . Brownlow, therefore, had his meals brought into the jail three times a day, and in sufficient amounts to take care of the wants of two Baptist preachers—to such humility or heroism had the distempers of the times reduced the Parson that

he was found providing food for and eating with Baptist preachers! Each day in the jail there were scenes of terror, heroism, and touching fortitude, as old and young were pushed in or sent out on their way to the prison at Tuscaloosa—or . . . to be executed.[7]

At different times, Brownlow feared that he would be executed, but after one month in jail, he was released and placed under house arrest for eight weeks. On March 3, 1862, on orders from Judah P. Benjamin, the Confederate secretary of war, Brownlow was banished to Union territory. The relative leniency shown to Brownlow was in large measure the result of his popularity and influence in east Tennessee—and the fear of the Confederacy in making a martyr of the man. During his residency in the North, Brownlow changed his mind on slavery and supported emancipation, though he would never view Blacks as social equals. In the fall of 1863, Brownlow returned to Tennessee with Burnside's army and once again became a leader among the Unionists in the eastern portion of the state. In 1865, he became governor of Tennessee and, during his tenure, sought to disfranchise those who had fought against the Union. As governor, Brownlow continually battled the Ku Klux Klan, which became a formidable force in the state.

Though Brownlow, as nearly as can be determined, did not participate in the burning of bridges, an east Tennessee clergyman who did was the Reverend William B. Carter, a Unionist from Carter County. Carter had journeyed to Washington where he met with President Lincoln and Major General George McClellan. The minister offered to assist a planned northern invasion of east Tennessee by destroying several vital railroad bridges that would cut off the major supply routes to Confederate forces. Carter's offer was approved by the president. Though the invasion was canceled, Carter and other east Tennessee Unionists, on the night of November 8, 1861, burned down five important railroad bridges and cut down several telegraph wires. These acts of sabotage greatly disrupted Confederate troop and supply movements in and out of east Tennessee, as well as leaving the troops in that area isolated because of their inability to establish communications with others. "Local secessionists feared for their lives," Noel Fisher has summarized, "and even Confederate officers were disoriented."[8]

To a lesser degree, there was also dissent in western Tennessee. A leading spokesman who protested against secession in this western area was the Reverend R. C. Grundy, minister of the Second Presbyterian Church in Memphis. Though at first silent on the issue, Grundy eventually became an outspoken, eloquent, and passionate proponent of loyalty to the United States. "He vigorously attacked disunion and all who believed in it. Those who heard such men as Grundy were often reduced to tears and sadness when they contemplated the choice before their state." Though most in western Tennessee had been converted to secession by the spring of 1861, Grundy would not change and "continued to hurl angry words at the secessionists." It was a daring stance, for there was "a band of the sons of Belial[9] [who] threaten tar and feathers" to Union sympathizers.

The only religious group that consistently and unanimously opposed slavery from colonial times through the Civil War was the Quakers. Carl N. Degler in commenting as to how few voices, individually or collectively, there were in the South that raised a moral protest against slavery notes, however, that there were exceptions. "A highly moral attack on slavery and slaveholders that came close at times to the position mounted by the extreme Northern abolitionists can be found among a few Southerners, particularly among Quakers." Between 1800 and 1830, there was a significant Quaker migration from the South, because these sensitive people found it too painful to live in the midst of the "peculiar institution" of slavery. They also were becoming increasingly aware that there was little else they could do, that their protests against slavery were being ignored by the dominant culture. Clement Eaton has written that "the passing of the antislavery Quakers from the South removed a vigorous element of dissent, and thus weakened the cause of free speech and a free press." One who did not migrate, but carried on in Virginia the traditional Quaker opposition to slavery, was the Quaker minister of the Hicksite sect, Samuel McPherson Janney. Eaton's appraisal of Janney was that he was "a universal reformer like Garrison, but with a better balanced mind."[10]

In 1826, Janney organized a group composed mostly of Quakers and a few Methodists, in Alexandria, Virginia, for the purpose of spreading antislavery sentiment in the area. The following year, he began to publish antislavery articles in the Alexandria *Gazette*. In these articles, he emphasized the necessity of being able to openly discuss slavery. Such openness, he was sure, would lead to the demise of the institution. His "strongest objection" to slavery, he wrote, was that "it degrades men by regarding them as property, and not only as property, but as *chattels personal*." Even in medieval serfdom, he attested, "family ties were not liable to be broken at the will of the master."[11]

Janney also noted that slavery, if continued, would lead the South into economic ruin. In the early 1840s, some New England farmers had come to Fairfax County in Virginia and purchased land, with the intent of instituting new farming methods. These Yankee farmers introduced crop rotation to the county and, using only white free labor, became very successful and prosperous. Janney pointed to the success of these immigrants from the North to bolster his claims as to the feasibility of free labor. His articles, entitled "The Yankees in Fairfax County," were published in the Richmond *Whig* and the Alexandria *Gazette*.[12]

Janney was a strong proponent for better educational standards in Virginia for both Blacks and Whites. He worked for the establishment of free schools in the state because, he claimed, the ignorance in Virginia was so great, especially when compared to the enlightened northern states. He complained that "seldom do we hear of a book being written by a Virginian! How few scientific discoveries we have made." Free schools, he announced, would promote "antislavery sentiment which was obstructed by ignorance and prejudice." During the 1850s, Moncure Conway and Janney joined in petitioning the Virginia legislature to rescind its law that made it illegal to teach slaves to read. The legislature refused to repeal the law.[13]

In the summer of 1850, Janney was indicted by the grand jury of Loudoun County for publishing an article that his accusers claimed "was calculated to incite persons of color to make insurrection or rebellion." The indictment was thrown out on a legal technicality. The grand jury indicted him a second time, this time for denying that "owners had right of property in their slaves." In his defense, Janney announced: "The longer you keep this subject before the people, the more there will be of my way of thinking." He argued his case on the basis of technicalities of the law and principles of constitutional liberty. So effective was Janney in his arguments to a jury composed mostly of slaveholders, that the charges against him were quashed. The judge, however, sternly lectured Janney on the importance of using great caution when addressing the sensitive issue of slavery. Eaton has noted that Janney was "a striking example of how much freedom a native Virginian with tact and estimable character could actually enjoy in expressing his opinions on slavery." During the war years, Janney stayed on in Virginia, where he not only continued his protest against slavery but also supported the Union. In his home, he cared for the wounded of both armies and aided his afflicted neighbors regardless of their sympathies."[14]

The Quakers, though they were the largest religious group in mid-nineteenth-century America to officially oppose war of any kind, were not alone in their conscientious objection to war. They were joined by the Mennonites, the German Baptist Brethren (Dunkers), the Shakers, the Amana Society, the Schwenkfelders, the Christadelphians, and the Rogerians. The Quakers in the North were faced with a real dilemma in the Civil War. They hated slavery and longed for its abolishment, yet war, which they also disdained, seemed to be the only means of emancipation. On September 4, 1864, President Lincoln wrote to his long-time Quaker friend, Eliza P. Gurney, informing her that he understood the dilemma the war had put upon the Quakers.

> Your people—the Friends—have had, and are having, a very great trial. On principle, and faith, opposed to both war and oppression, they can practically oppose oppression by war. In this hard dilemma, some have chosen one horn and some the other. For those appealing to me on conscientious grounds, I have done, and shall do, the best I could and can, in my own conscience, under my oath to the law. That you believe this I doubt not; and believing it, I shall still receive, for our country, and myself, your earnest prayers to our Father in Heaven.[15]

The Quakers and other conscientious objectors were treated well in the North, and for the most part, their lot in the South was tolerable. However, notes Edward Needles Wright, "during the war Southern objectors were generally subjected to greater trials than were those in the North partly because of the shortage of fighting men in the Confederacy." Also, President Jefferson Davis was not as sympathetic toward religious objectors as was President Lincoln. There are several accounts of severe treatment administered to pacifists in the South, mostly by military authorities who resented the idea that there were some who felt themselves exempt from fighting and war. There are documented accounts of conscientious objectors in the South who were forced to flee to the safety of the North and others who were imprisoned and threatened with death. One particular incident of unusually harsh treatment was that given to a Quaker, Seth W. Laughlin, who was arrested and taken to a military camp near Petersburg, Virginia. There, military authorities attempted to force Laughlin to give up his religious objections to war.

First they kept him without sleep for thirty-six hours, a soldier standing by with a bayonet to pierce him, should he fall asleep. Finding that this did not overcome his scruples, they proceeded for three hours each day to buck him down. He was then suspended by his thumbs for an hour and a half. This terrible ordeal was passed through with each day for a week. Then, thinking him conquered, they offered him a gun; but he was unwilling to use the weapon. Threats, abuse and persecution were alike unavailing, and in desperate anger the Colonel ordered him court-martialed. After being tried for insubordination he was ordered shot. Preparations were accordingly made for the execution of this terrible sentence. The army was summoned to witness the scene, and soldiers were detailed. Guns, six loaded with bullets and six without, were handed to twelve chosen men. Seth Laughlin, as calm as any man of the immense number surrounding him, asked time for prayer, which, of course, could not be denied him. The supposition was natural that he wished to pray for himself. But he was ready to meet his Lord; and so he prayed not for himself but for them: "Father, forgive them, for they know not what they do."

Strange was the effect of this familiar prayer upon men used to taking human life and under strict military orders. Each man, however, lowered his gun, and they resolutely declared that they would not shoot such a man, thereby braving the result of disobeying military orders. But the chosen twelve were not the only ones whose hearts were touched.

The officers themselves revoked the sentence, and he was led away to prison, where for weeks he suffered uncomplainingly from his severe punishments. He was finally sent to Windsor Hospital at Richmond, Virginia, where he was taken very sick, and after a long, severe illness . . . he passed quietly away, leaving a wife and seven children.[16]

Wright observes that when the entire picture is taken into account, "it is apparent that the cases of extreme severity in the South [toward conscientious objectors] were the exception rather than the rule. Where such cases did occur, the responsibility for harsh treatment usually rested on the shoulders of subordinate officers and not on those of the higher officers or the privates."[17]

Other dissenting clergy in Virginia included a Universalist minister from Richmond, who was arrested and imprisoned because he prayed for Abraham Lincoln; John T. Clark, an Episcopal rector from Halifax County, who, although he was the owner of 150 slaves, was labeled an abolitionist and forced to leave the ministry because he was considered a Unionist; and M. R. Watkins, pastor of the Court Street Baptist Church in Portsmouth, who was expelled by his congregation, rather than being allowed to resign, for his Union sympathies.[18]

North Carolina also had her share of dissenting clergy. In 1861, the North Carolina Methodist Conference struck a minister from its rolls for his allegiance to the Union, condemning him as "a traitor to his Conference, his State, and the Southern Confederacy." As the war neared its end, another Methodist minister, Marble Nash Taylor, was accused of giving information to federal authorities, which made Union conquest easier. He and another man went to a meeting in New York, which was presided over by George Bancroft, a historian, at which plans were formulated for setting up a new state government in North Carolina. Taylor would later protest that he was forced by circumstances to cooperate with the Union.[19]

Taylor belonged to one of the several peace societies that began to emerge throughout the South due to disaffection with the war. The societies began to greatly proliferate in 1863 as enthusiasm for secession and war seriously eroded. The length of the war, the feeling of many that the war was for the benefit of the wealthy slaveowners, the great suffering being experienced by soldiers and civilians, the impressment of supplies by the Confederate armies—

all these discomforts led to an increasing disillusionment with the Confederate cause. "In Alabama, Arkansas, Georgia, Texas, and Mississippi there existed a disloyal chain of organizations known as the 'Peace Society,' and in Virginia, Tennessee, North Carolina, and perhaps South Carolina, disloyal societies known as 'Heroes of America.'" Frank Owsley has written that "the purposes of the 'Peace Society' and the 'Heroes of America' were the same: to bring about peace by submission to the Federal government." Though most clergy members implored the South to fight on, whatever the odds, no matter how bleak and hopeless the circumstances appeared, there were a few ministers in the South, like Taylor, who became active in one of the various peace societies.[20]

Membership in a peace society was secretive. "On entering the society a member was sworn to absolute secrecy on the penalty of having 'his head cut open . . . brains taken out . . . and strewn over the ground and . . . body cast to the beasts of the field.' The society neither individually nor collectively was permitted to keep any kind of record and it was very difficult to verify members."[21] There were secret passwords and signs. If it was discovered that one belonged to such a subversive organization, dangerous consequences could result. To lessen the consequences upon exposure of belonging to a peace society, a member would often plead that he was forced into joining or had joined without being informed as to what the organization was really all about. It will be recalled that Marble Nash Taylor made such a plea. Another North Carolina minister whose membership in a peace society was revealed was the Reverend Orin Churchill of Caswell County who signed a confession that he had belonged to the Order of Heroes of America. Georgia Lee Tatum has written of some who signed such confessions.

> Confessions were made by many men who claimed that they did not mean to be disloyal but that they had been induced to join the order because they wanted

protection for themselves, but particularly for their families, from the Federals in case the latter invaded North Carolina. Most of the men withdrawing from the society said that they had been induced to join by a member whom they considered a friend. They had been told that the organization would furnish them certain information useful to them and their families in case the Federals overran their section. No one had told them that, when they were members, they were supposed to give information to the Federals in return for the protection promised. Neither did they understand that, in order to receive the information and aid promised, the Federals must in some way be connected with the society so as to be able to respond to the appeal for help and protection. Some of the members claimed they were not told, even after they joined, that they must give information to the enemy and work against the Confederacy.[22]

In July 1861, the Reverend Eli Washington Caruthers of Greensboro, North Carolina, prayed before his congregation that the young men serving in the Confederate Army "might be blessed of the Lord and return in safety though engaged in a bad cause." For this public expression of disloyalty, Caruthers was dismissed from his church. It had been suspected for some time that Caruthers was opposed to slavery, but because he had chosen to keep silent on the subject, he was retained by his congregation. In 1842, Caruthers had noted the trend toward conformity in his state. He observed that books by Voltaire, Hobbes, and Paine—books generally disapproved of for their skepticism in North Carolina—though available and openly read in the earlier years of the century, had been burned or hidden so that copies were now nearly impossible to locate. In a way, Caruthers had contributed to the conformity by maintaining silence on an issue he considered of paramount importance—slavery.

His strong antislavery views had been formulated when

he was a student at Princeton. By the time of his dismissal from his church in 1861, Caruthers had, for a number of years, been working on an antislavery manuscript. This treatise, nearly 400 pages in length, entitled "American Slavery and the Immediate Duty of Slaveholders," was never published. In the manuscript's preface, Caruthers explained: "The following work would have been published years ago, but for the last fifteen years its publication or circulation would not have been tolerated in any of the Southern States."[23]

This never-published manuscript was as sophisticated a polemic against slavery as could be found in the United States, North or South, in the middle years of the nineteenth century. A few excerpts will demonstrate the profundity of Caruther's argument.

> According to the ablest and best writers on Ethnology, the south sea islands are a more degraded people than even the Caffres [*sic*] and Hottentots; and therefore, by parity of reasoning, they are the people that ought to be enslaved, but this has not been noticed by the slaveholders. If this most degraded are not to be enslaved why should those in the next stage above them be thus treated? Where is there any authority in such a proceeding? . . . For long generations [the Negroes] appear to have been the superior race and to be the admiration of the literary and scientific community, the mutilated and long buried monuments of their greatness have been brought to light on the Nile, the Tigris and the Euphrates. . . . Should we not honor them as a race for what they have done and for what God has done for them and by them? And it surely does not become us to treat them thus with contempt and rigor without a cause, for our ancestors were once very little if any better than the Caffres or Hottentots of the present day. . . . Even if they were as inferior as the advocates of slavery assert, they certainly have as good a right to the free use of whatever power the creator has given them as the weak-minded among the whites or as those who be more liberally endowed.[24]

Other clergy dissenters in North Carolina included R. J. Graves, a Presbyterian minister from Orange County, who was arrested in the fall of 1862 on charges of treason. He was accused of writing a letter that gave encouragement to federal authorities. Acquitted of the charges, he was allowed to return to his home, though he was a confessed Unionist. The Reverend James Sinclair, born in Scotland, had come to North Carolina a few years before the outbreak of the Civil War. Though a slaveholder, Sinclair opposed secession, a stance that would culminate in the loss of his church and arrest during the war. In testimony before Congress on January 29, 1866, Sinclair spoke of the treatment he had received during the war and the fact that dissenters were still mistreated in North Carolina even after the war's end.

> I for one would not wish to be left there in the hands of those men; I could not live there just now. But perhaps my case is an isolated one from the position I was compelled to take in that State. I was persecuted, arrested, and they tried to get me into their service; they tried everything to accomplish their purpose, and of course I have rendered myself still more obnoxious by accepting an appointment under the Freedmen's Bureau. As for myself I would not be allowed to remain there. I do not want to be handed over to those people. I know it is utterly impossible for any man who was not true to the Confederate States up to the last moment of the existence of the confederacy, to expect any favor of these people as the State is constituted at present.[25]

In the lower South, the dissenting clergy were fewer in number, but they did exist; and the consequences they paid for their nonconformity were sometimes severe. There were, of course, those who were dismissed from their churches, and/or forced to leave the South. In Mississippi, there was a young clergyman by the name of Galladet, who had recently been ordained to the Presbyterian ministry. At a presbytery meeting, Galladet drew a severe rebuke from an older minister when the young cleric suggested that there would be no slavery in the millennium. The senior minister replied that slavery would continue to exist in some modified form in heaven. "Southern people," he attested, "would require slaves in heaven in order to promote their highest happiness." Galladet became the pastor of the Presbyterian church in Aberdeen, where he found bitter opposition to his views on slavery and his pro-Unionist sympathies. After a short time, he was compelled to abandon his church and escape to the North in order to save his life. In Copiah County, Mississippi, the Reverend George B. Mortimer's loyalty to the Union resulted in social ostracism for his family and the endangering of his own life.[26]

Soon after the war began, a civil war in miniature broke out between the Episcopal bishop for Texas, Alexander Gregg, and a clergyman of his diocese, the rector of St. David's Church in Austin, Charles Gillette. The seeds of trouble were actually sown in 1856 when a Unionist faction in Austin's Church of the Epiphany broke away and formed Christ Church. The new congregation called Connecticut-born Charles Gillette, a rector in Houston, to be its pastor. Christ Church, under Gillette's leadership, more than doubled its membership in the next few years. In July 1859, the two Episcopal congregations reunited. The merged congregations took upon themselves a new name, St. David's, with Gillette as pastor.

In the fall of 1860, the intensifying sectional crisis brought new tensions to St. David's, which had divided over similar issues just four years before. The states' righters from the old Church of the Epiphany were a part of the congregation, as were those who had demonstrated their loyalty to the Union by organizing Christ Church. Gillette, who could not be neutral, sided with the Unionist contingent. This brought him into conflict not only with some of the members of his congregation, but also with his bishop, Alexander Gregg, a passionate advocate of secession and the Confederacy. Shortly after the firing on Fort Sumter in the spring of 1861, Gregg ordered the clergy of his diocese to change the liturgy in order that it might better conform to the new military and political situation. Gillette thought that the new prescribed prayer "savored far too strong of party feeling for public use in the church." However, the rector felt that he could, in good conscience, repeat the prayer, except for the phrase that asked for a speedy end to "the unnatural war which has been forced upon us." He vehemently opposed the phrase and plainly stated his unwillingness to repeat it. "When it comes to the mere assertion of fact," he announced, "concerning which there was a great difference of opinion—an assertion which I did not believe to be true, as a matter of fact—I did not think it right for me to make it."[27]

For a time, the bishop, seeking harmony in his diocese, allowed Gillette to omit the offending phrase; but as the war progressed, emotions intensified and opinions polarized, and the few words became, for the bishop and others of his diocese, a test of loyalty to matters that were dear and even sacred.

For the next few years an all-out battle between the rector of St. David's and his bishop was enjoined. A series of letters went back and forth between the two strong-willed individuals. The letters, though accusatory and uncompromising in nature, were properly polite. They began, "My Dear Bishop," and "Brother Gillette." The bishop wrote of the importance of obedience to superiors in the structure of the Episcopal Church, of the North's infidelity and disobedience to the Scriptures in attacking slavery, and of the importance of national loyalty to the Confederacy. Gillette argued that Gregg had overstepped the limits of his authority and that the bishop had proclaimed as truth that which only God could know.[28]

Gillette was fighting a battle he could not win, however. Unionists in his congregation were intimidated. At least one was arrested; another's house was burned. Gillette's allies in the congregation were reduced to silence or left the state. In early August 1864, Bishop Gregg ordered an end to the letters between himself and Gillette. "The correspondence is at an end," he wrote. "Enough has been said, the argument is virtually exhausted." Gregg's brief letter ended: "As your Bishop, [I] will add one warning word . . . weigh well the course upon which you have entered, as it only seems to be leading you, in spirit, from one degree of insubordination to another." The letter was signed, "Yours in the Church, Alex Gregg."[29]

In the same month, a vestry committee of St. David's requested Gillette's resignation. On October 1, the pastor complied:

> Gentlemen: Circumstances connected with the singular course pursued by the Bishop of the Diocese towards myself, make it expedient that I should resign. . . . I am happy to feel assured that a majority, both of the Vestry and of the congregation, have been and are still satisfied with my ministrations; and in reality, desire no change.[30]

On August 10, 1864, Gillette wrote a rather lengthy letter to Gregg in which he outlined his differences with the bishop. The letter was never sent because Gregg had forbidden further communication. A few sentences from the unsent letter illustrate how greatly the relationship between the two men had deteriorated.

> I contend you have ordered that which is contrary to Canon, and the question is, when a superior orders an inferior to break what he believes a plain law, may he (the inferior) obey and be guiltless? . . . I think the South threatened war first, and finally chose it and commenced it, as a way of deciding a political difference. . . . To this opinion . . . I had a right, and neither you, nor the Council, had any right . . . to deprive me of it. . . . What Pope of Rome every required greater obedience to his infallible mandate? Was not freedom of conscience one of the main points contended for in the Reformation? . . .

This whole matter may now be summed up in a few
words. It is evident, from all our correspondence, that
my offense (very grievous in your eyes) has been that I
did not sympathize so deeply with the Southern Confederacy, as you thought I ought to do.[31]

Gillette was unable to collect $1500, which the church
owed him after his resignation. Therefore, he, his wife,
and their six children, because of their lack of financial re-
sources, were forced to remain in Austin. In July 1865,
the war having concluded, Gillette was recalled to the pastorate of St. David's. In October, he left St. David's to
accept a call to a parish in Steubenville, Ohio. Upon his
leaving, the vestrymen of St. David's passed a resolution
that stated that during his rectorship of the church, the
Reverend Mr. Gillette had "faithfully, honestly, conscien-
tiously discharged his duties," and they expressed "admira-
tion for his excellence as a citizen, gentleman and
Christian."[32]

Another Unionist who had trouble in Texas was New
Englander Melinda Rankin who came to Brownsville in
1852 to begin missionary work among the Mexican population of that community. She immediately began a school
for children, which experienced rapid growth. Two years
later, she and her students moved into a newly constructed
facility, the Rio Grande Female Seminary, built from funds
donated by various Protestant groups in the North, especially the Presbyterian Board of Education in Philadelphia.
In September 1862, a Presbyterian minister with whom
she worked sent her a written notice "to vacate the build-
ing, and deliver up the keys of the same." When Rankin
replied that she did not wish to give up her work and asked
why she should, the minister, in another written statement,
replied: "You are not in sympathy with the Southern Confederacy, and no teachers but such as are can be permitted
to occupy that institution." The note continued: "You are
in communication with a country that is called the United
States." When Rankin protested again, the minister sent a

third letter that intimated that if she did not leave voluntarily, then she would be expelled by force.[33] Rankin fled across the river into Mexico where she taught school in Matamoros for the next year. She then went on to New Orleans, which at that time was occupied by federal troops, and there she nursed Union troops in the hospital and conducted a school for freedmen. In 1864, she followed Union troops back into Brownsville, rebuilt her school, and resumed her work. When the federal authorities abandoned the Rio Grande area, Rankin was once again compelled to leave Brownsville and return to New Orleans. She never again resumed her work in Brownsville.

In her memoir, Rankin wrote of a Reverend James Hickey, a colporteur (a distributor of religious materials) of the American Tract Society for Texas, who, because of his Union leanings, "was obliged to flee to Mexico to preserve his life, as all persons in the South had to do at that time, who were loyal to the Government of the United States."[34]

Most Presbyterian clergy members in Texas would have been in sympathy with the stance taken by the minister who notified Melinda Rankin that she must vacate her school and turn in her keys, but not all of them. A Presbyterian of a different stripe was Thaddeus McRae, who, though born and nurtured in the South (South Carolina and Mississippi), believed secession to be unconstitutional and let his views be known. Such a conviction alienated him from his congregation in Louisiana, and he accepted a call from a church in Port Lavaca, Texas, thinking the Lone Star State was surely outside the "region temporarily abandoned by God to its own devices." He had resided in Texas for only a short time when he discovered that "there I was again with a bastard flag, floating over me." As the war continued and emotions intensified, the efforts of McRae's congregation in Port Lavaca to stave off the local vigilance committee weakened, and McRae was forced to seek refuge behind Union lines in New Orleans, where he joined the Union army under General Benjamin Butler and became a chaplain of a black regiment.

A special committee of the presbytery, appointed to investigate the McRae incident, issued the following statement some months after McRae had fled to New Orleans.

> Whereas it has come to the knowledge of this Presbytery through what we conceive to be reliable authority, that our heretofore respected and dear brother, Rev. Thad. McRae, has forsaken his flock and gone into the Federal lines, under circumstances calculated to destroy his usefulness within our bounds, and being (a) reproach upon the cause of Christ, therefore, Resolved, "That we record our disapprobation of his course, expressing the hope that he may yet confess his fault, until which, his name shall be omitted from our roll."

Upon review of the statement, the synod caused the presbytery to strike out the clause "and gone into the Federal lines."[35] Apparently, McRae's reputation was not irreparably damaged, for after the war, he returned to Texas and pastored a Presbyterian church in Austin. In the Texas Constitutional Convention of 1865, McRae was elected chaplain of that body, and a few months later, he was made the private secretary to Governor E. M. Pease.[36] McRae's positions during the Reconstruction era most likely came to him as one later defined as a "scalawag."

In every state representing the lower South, Unionist clergy were expelled from their pulpits and/or fled to the North in order to live among those more in accord with their views. David Young, a Methodist lay preacher in Atlanta, Georgia, was accused of being an abolitionist because of his Union sympathies and was expelled from his church. Soon after the war began, the Reverend Charles W. Thomas, of the Georgia Methodist Conference, moved to the North and joined the Methodist Episcopal Church. He eventually served as a chaplain in the Union army. In Jacksonville, Florida, the Reverend Horatio H. Hewitt, pastor of St. John's Episcopal Church, fled to the North in 1862.[37]

In Arkansas, one of the last states to join the Confederacy, opposition to secession was rampant throughout the war. Peace societies were organized as early as 1861, and ministers were active participants in these societies. Baptist clergymen Solomon Branum, H. W. Davis, George Long, and Joshua Reeves and Methodist ministers John M. Carithers and Joshua Richardson were active in the organization of and soliciting membership for the Arkansas Peace Society.[38]

Some dissident clergy discovered that nonconformity resulted in more than expulsion from a church or banishment to the North. Disloyalty, viewed as treason, often resulted in imprisonment. Captain John Geer of the Union army was taken prisoner during the battle of Shiloh in the spring of 1862 and imprisoned in Columbus, Mississippi. Geer related that also confined in the same place were "a number of political prisoners. . . . about one hundred and fifty Mississippi citizens, such as were suspected of Union sentiments in a most loathsome situation." Among those imprisoned citizens "were three clergymen—one a Presbyterian, one a 'United Brother,' and the other a Methodist."[39]

Ministers discovered that they could be imprisoned for failures of omission as well as commission. On May 17, 1862, Brigadier General C. D. Dahlgren, a commander in Fayette, Mississippi, wrote a letter to Brigadier General Thomas Jordan, the assistant adjutant general at Corinth. Dahlgren complained that one of his chief concerns was the lack of support for the war that some of the people in the area were demonstrating: "conscripts who refuse to serve," and those who were "disaffected, at least wavering in their support." He noted that the Fayette County jail held dissidents who were awaiting their trial, among them "a minister of the Gospel, who on the fast day of Friday, as ordered by President Davis, refused or omitted to pray for the President of the Confederate States."

On May 25, General P. G. T. Beauregard replied to Dahlgren's letter. He emphasized that "I duly approve

and commend your course in arresting disloyal citizens."
However, he continued, "as to the minister of the Gospel,
I would not interfere with him so long as he does not preach
obedience to Northern rule and does nothing contrary to
Confederate laws."[40]

Perhaps the best-known dissident clergyman who was
imprisoned was the Presbyterian evangelist from Mississippi,
the Reverend John H. Aughey, who ministered in Choctaw
and Attala counties in central Mississippi. Aughey wrote of
his experiences, which included imprisonment and the sentence of death for his Union sentiments. His suspenseful
and sometimes terrifying narration caused his account to
receive a wide reading, most especially, as might be expected,
in the northern states.[41]

In December 1860, after the election of Lincoln to
the presidency, and after South Carolina had become the
first southern state to secede from the Union, but before
Mississippi had taken a similar step, Aughey delivered a sermon in which he directly addressed the secession crisis.
Taking his text from Romans 13:1—"Let every soul be
subject unto the higher powers. . . . The powers that be are
ordained of God"—Aughey declared: "Loyalty to the government is obedience to God, for God has commanded
it." Referring to the election of Lincoln, which brought
the secession crisis to a head, Aughey exclaimed: "The late
presidential election was conducted under a strict observance of all forms of the Constitution. It was participated
in by all the states—even belligerent South Carolina held
an election with protest. . . . Should we repudiate a result
in which by voting we have made ourselves parties?"[42]

Aughey affirmed that a national government in which
various so-called independent and sovereign parties could
nullify laws, or even secede if a major dispute arose, would
be "a rope of sand without cohesion." Such a government,
the preacher announced, "is inefficient and powerless for
good . . . unworthy of respect, wholly at the mercy of demagogues, the scorn, derision, and contempt of all stable gov-
ernments . . . a bubble ready to burst at any moment."[43]

The preacher declared that there need not be a conflict between state and national authority.

> I believe in state sovereignty. I believe also in national supremacy. . . . States rights as distinguished from national authority has been a dangerous and disturbing element in American politics. . . . Their functions pertain to different spheres and in their exercise there is no conflict and needs be none. Let us love our state with an ardent love and our sister states with an equal love, for we are all children of our common parent, the government of the United States.[44]

Aughey castigated South Carolina for her secessionist actions. "South Carolina," he exclaimed, "has usurped the prerogative of the supreme court. Her action is unconstitutional and void, and may result in a bloody, fratricidal civil war." He urged Mississippi not to follow "supremely silly and superlatively wicked South Carolina! Let us not imitate her folly and thus become partaker of her sin and consequent punishment if she should carry to a logical conclusion the initiatory act of treason and rebellion against the nation and her own true interests."[45]

Mississippi, however, did follow the example of South Carolina. It then became dangerous, exclaimed Aughey, "to utter a word in favor of the Union. Many suspected of Union sentiments were lynched. . . . Self-constituted vigilante committees sprang up all over the country, and a reign of terror began."[46]

Aughey was summoned to appear before a vigilance committee, a committee consisting of twelve persons, five known to Aughey. The Reverend John Locke, a Methodist, was "the chief speaker, or rather the inquisitor-general." Also on the committee was W. H. Simpson, "a ruling elder in my church," and Armstrong, "a monocular Hardshell-Baptist." The committee charged Aughey with "holding abolitionist sentiments" and "being disloyal to the Confederate States." The issue was raised of Aughey's birth and education in the North. He was asked: "Parson Aughey, are you in favor of the South?" Aughey replied:

> I am in favor of the South, and have always endeav-
> ored to promote the best interests of the South. How-
> ever, I never deemed it for the best interests of the South
> to secede. I talked against secession and voted against
> secession, because I thought that the best interests of the
> South would be put in jeopardy by the secession of the
> Southern States. I was honest in my convictions, and
> acted accordingly. Could the sacrifice of my life have
> stayed the swelling tide of secession, it would gladly have
> been made.[47]

The committee temporarily adjourned, and for the next few days, Aughey was terrorized. There were threats of death. His home was raided. Attempts were made to do him physical harm, and a notice of his death appeared in the local newspaper. He attempted to escape to the safety of the North but was captured, charged with sedition, and imprisoned at Tupelo, Mississippi. Aughey described the conditions of the prison.

> The prison was filthy in the extreme, and full of
> vermin, even our food was infested. . . . No beds or
> bedding were provided. . . . Where we lay the floor was
> saturated with molasses. When I tried to rise in the
> morning I could not. My coat was apparently hermeti-
> cally fastened to the floor. . . . On the evening succeeding
> our incarceration two prisoners had been led out and
> shot. . . . Nearly every day one or more suffered death as
> the punishment of their patriotism. Many of the prison-
> ers wore heavy fetters on their ankles, and were chained
> to bolts in the floor.[48]

Aughey resolved to escape, and did, but was recap-
tured. Charged with treason and spying for the Union, the minister was sentenced to death. He wrote a final let-

ter to his wife and prepared the speech he would deliver just before his death.[49] Before the sentence could be carried out, however, Aughey escaped once more, and this time made it to safety behind Union lines. He carried with him a petition to Secretary of State William H. Seward. The petition, written by Aughey on July 11, 1862, at the Central Military Prison at Tupelo, and signed by thirty-seven fellow prisoners, said in part:

> A large number of citizens of Mississippi holding Union sentiments and who recognize no such military usurpation as the so-called Confederate States of America are confined in a filthy prison swarming with vermin and are famishing from hunger, a sufficient quantity of food not being furnished us. We are separated from our families and suffered to hold no communication with them. . . . Our property is confiscated and our families destitute of the necessities of life, all that we have, yea, all their living, being seized upon by the Confederates and converted to their own use. . . . The Federal Government may not be able to release us, but we ask protection which the Federal prisoner receives. Were his life taken swift retribution would be visited upon the rebels by a just retaliation; a rebel prisoner would suffer death for every Federal prisoner whom they destroyed. Let this rule hold good in the case of Union men who are citizens of the South. The loyal Mississippian deserves protection as much as the loyal native of Massachusetts. We ask also that our confiscated property be restored to us or in case of our death to our families. . . . The writer has been informed by the officers that "his chances for living long are very slender;" that he has confessed enough to cause him to lose his life, and the judge-advocate has specified Tuesday, the 15th instant, as the day of his execution. We have therefore little hope that we individually can receive any benefit from this petition, though you regard it favorably and consent to its suggestions, but our families who have been so cruelly robbed of all their substance may after time receive remuneration for their great losses. And if citizens of avowed secession proclivi-

ties who are within the Federal lines are arrested and held
as hostages for the safety of Union men who are many
may hereafter be incarcerated in prison in Tupelo and
elsewhere the rebels will not dare to put another Union
man to death.[50]

In November 1862, writing in the *New York Independent*, the noted journalist Horace Greeley summarized the
story of Aughey's imprisonment and escape.

> Arrested as a traitor to the treason whereto he had
> never actively nor passively adhered, and which he
> therefore could not betray, he was heavily manacled and
> thrust into a crowded, filthy prison, where his compan-
> ions were taken out day by day to be shot, and their
> bodies thrown naked into a ditch as punishment for their
> patriotism. Mr. Aughey himself, as a more determined
> and influential Unionist, was reserved for conspicuous
> hanging, but escaped before the fulfillment of that
> amiable intention. Traveling in the opposite direction
> from that in which he would naturally be sought, wearing
> on his ankles the heavy iron fetters which he had not
> been enabled to remove, he was obliged to evade the
> blood-hounds that are usually kept for the hunting of
> slaves, but now employed for tracking white Unionists,
> taking care to leave none of his garments in the prison, as
> from these the scent might be taken; traveling only by
> night, and then very slowly because of the falling circlets
> of his ankles; living mainly on green corn plucked from
> the field and eaten raw, since to raise a smoke would have
> been to advertise his location to watchful, unrelenting
> foes; he finally discovered himself at a venture to a farmer
> who proved a Unionist, and by whom he was conveyed
> on horseback several miles in the right direction, and thus
> enabled to evade the Rebel pickets and find refuge under
> the protecting folds of the Flag of Freedom. . . . Mr.
> Aughey's conclusion from all he had seen and heard is,
> that the number of those who have been murdered in the
> South for their loyalty—some of them black, but by far
> the greater portion white—is really appalling.[51]

Some ministers in the Confederacy, such as James Pelan, pastor of the Presbyterian church in Macon, Mississippi, paid for their nonconformity with their lives. Because of his Unionist sentiment, a committee of citizens examined Pelan's library, where they discovered some volumes that contained abolitionist ideas. Though he tried to be discreet in his preaching, his sermons were misconstrued, and he was accused of conveying heresies and treasons that he never proclaimed. Citizens threatened to lynch him. Tiring of such intimidations, Pelan resigned his pastorate and moved to a country home. His enemies pursued him. One evening, while walking near his home, he was fired upon by hidden assassins. For many days, he hovered between life and death and then began a slow recovery. Those who had attempted to kill him learned that they had failed in their task and planned to remedy the situation. Late one afternoon at about suppertime, Pelan was eating when three men came to his house and asked for something to eat. Mrs. Pelan replied, "Certainly," and then left the room to give orders for further supper preparations. The three men then arose and one of them said to the minister, "All the supper we want is to kill you, you infernal Unionist and abolitionist." Then, all three men fired bullets into the defenseless clergyman. Pelan's wife, upon hearing the shots, burst into the room and held her husband in her arms for the last few moments of his life. The dying Pelan whispered, "Father, forgive them, they know not what they do." Then, "Farewell, dear wife, I die but the government still lives and will eventually subvert rebellion, for God is just." His last words were: "Lord Jesus, receive my spirit."[52]

Not all dissenting clergy, however, even in the deep South, were dismissed from pulpits, forced to leave the South, imprisoned, or killed. There were a few ministers, a very few, who opposed secession and were still able to maintain their positions, although with some difficulties, throughout the war. As to how and why this was possible will be dealt with in the conclusion of this work. In Carroll County, Louisiana, an Episcopal minister, Frederick W.

Boyd, continued to pray for the president of the United
States, though his bishop, Leonidas K. Polk, had instructed
his clergy to omit such prayers from their worship services.
Milton S. Shirk, a Baptist minister from Shreveport, Louisiana, held on to his pastorate though he was a known
Unionist and refused to pray for Jefferson Davis. The most
notable example in this category was the Reverend James
A. Lyon, pastor of the First Presbyterian Church in Columbus, Mississippi, who "opposed secession, criticized
Davis, condemned the war as the work of demagogues, . . .
favored Reconstruction," and "somehow held the esteem
of his parishioners and, in 1863, was selected a moderator
of the Southern Presbyterian General Assembly."[53]

In 1861, Lyon was a delegate from the Presbytery of
Tombeckbee to the first General Assembly of the Confederate Presbyterian Church, held in Augusta, Georgia, where
he "was drawn into a leading part." By his own account,
he gave a speech "devoted to the consideration of the religious instruction of slaves," wherein he maintained "that
negro slavery . . . was not yet up to the Bible standard."
Partly because of this address, "which seemed to astonish
and delight the assembly," Lyon was appointed the chairman of a committee "to prepare a manifesto on slavery and
the religious instruction of negroes." The committee was
instructed to have its report ready for the next meeting of
the General Assembly in 1863.[54]

The finished report, written mostly if not entirely by
Lyon himself, was presented in an address by Lyon to the
General Assembly of 1863, meeting in Montgomery, Alabama. The report called for major revisions in the slave codes,
especially in the areas of education and the protection of
family relationships among the slaves. Called upon to defend the report in committee, Lyon declared that he "defended each and every part of it from beginning to
end—boldly and fearlessly—admonishing them that the
church . . . was not to consult Caesar, but Christ." The
assembly, apparently fearing adverse repercussions if the

report was adopted, never brought it to a vote, though Lyon was sure "that the Assembly was largely in favor of my address."[55] Though his report was not accepted, Lyon was, however, selected moderator of the assembly, a testimony of the esteem in which he was held even though his views were at variance with many, if not most, of the assembly delegates.

With the war only three months old, Lyon's congregation began to take steps to decrease his salary. Only after the minister threatened to resign did such efforts cease. It would seem that the attempt to lower Lyon's salary at that time was not due to congregational disfavor with their pastor but rather to the financial problems that churches throughout the Confederacy were experiencing.[56]

In 1862, Lyon felt compelled to preach a fast-day sermon at the community service in Columbus. The Baptist and Methodist ministers, for various reasons, were unable to preach the sermon, "so that there was no alternative left me but to preach on that occasion." Deciding not to preach on "smooth things," Lyon, in the sermon, blamed the southern people in general, and "their rulers" in particular for the "evils of the war," declaring that "the only hope was in repentance." During the sermon, some people in the congregation walked out, demonstrating "that they were offended" by the words and tone of Lyon's sermon.[57]

The rejection of his report to the General Assembly of the Confederate Presbyterian Church in 1863 was not the only rebuff Lyon suffered in that particular year. During the autumn of 1863, Lyon's son, Theodoric, an officer in the Confederate army, was brought before a court-martial in what appeared to be a means of indirectly attacking his father. Theodoric had invited the hatred and anger of ardent secessionists by writing a letter in which he defended the sentiments and views of his father. For this offense, the court-martial stripped him of his command and transferred him to Virginia, where he spent the remainder of the war vainly attempting to secure a pardon. In his journal, James

Lyon reflected upon the penalty imposed on his son.

> We are amazed at the result. Instead of an honorable
> acquittal, as we felt certain justice required—or a simple
> reprimand as the utmost limit of which they could go,
> influenced by the pressure of demagogues, it is one of the
> greatest severity and outrage—It is undoubtedly a
> sacrifice to policy. He is cashiered—conscripted and
> reduced to the ranks—separated from his regiment and
> sent to some regiment in Virginia under guard—and
> deprived of his back pay—amounting to about $700. . . .
> This is astonishing and unaccountable . . . and not in
> accordance with the law, testimony or conscience.[58]

At the same time Theodoric was being court-
martialed, he ran for the state legislature—an act that increased "the rage of the persecutors." The printer who
was to prepare circulars for Theodoric was threatened with
mob violence. After the circulars were finally printed, they
were pulled down soon after they were posted. At the polls,
"bullies stood around the box . . . marked on the ticket the
number of the voter, so that his ticket could be identified.
This deterred a large number from voting for Theodoric
that would otherwise have done so." Though Theodoric
lost the election, James Lyon proclaimed a moral victory:
"The vote cast in the town and country notwithstanding
these adverse circumstances was respectable—he getting in
town 74 votes, and altogether 156 in the county, which
was one fourth of the entire vote cast." Lyon found further consolation in the fact that "Mr. James Arnold who
was known to hold to conservative principles was elected
by a decided majority."[59] Lyon's journal seems to indicate
that there was considerable support for peace and sentiment against the war in his district.

In 1863, potential trouble for Lyon also developed in
his church. Lyon wrote, "Two or three rabid men in the
church and two or three violent men out of the church,

but directly or indirectly connected with the congregation, have been exceedingly outraged because I did not agree with them in their 'blood and thunder' politics, and preach and pray . . . to suit them." These men attempted to draw up a paper to present to Lyon protesting his political sentiments. The letter failed for lack of signatures. Lyon's enemies then attempted to have a congregational petition sent to the presbytery and synod, but only 9 out of the church's 180 members signed it. This congregational support for Lyon certainly confirmed his personal popularity with his congregation and may also have been an indication of a growing lack of support for secession and war. Lyon's descriptions of his enemies in this affair say much about the fire that burned in his own spirit. He depicted one a "perfectly unscrupulous demagogue, besides being a drunken scoffer and debauchee." Another, according to Lyon, "has failed in all the ends of his life." A third enemy was an "arch demagogue" who "felt that the scepter of his reign was passing away." "The rage of these men," Lyon wrote, "knew no bounds." With these failed attempts to remove him from his church, Lyon, after 1863, was left pretty much unmolested for the duration of the war.[60]

Early in 1865, Lyon lobbied to have the state legislature in Mississippi pass a bill that would recognize the inviolability of black marriages and prohibit the separation of slave children under twelve from their mothers. The proposed bill died in committee, where it was declared that public opinion would not as yet accept and comply with such legislation.[61]

At the end of the war, Lyon recorded his assessment of the civil conflict:

> This cruel war has at last ended by the complete subjugation of the South—or rather the leaders of the rebellion—for strictly speaking it was not a war of the people but a war of the demagogues who had subjugated and enslaved the people. . . . It originated in lies of the basest kind—it was kept up by lies its whole life, consisted of lies

promulgated systematically, and with malice-propense. . . . Among the multitudinous fallacies. . . .

"There will be no war, etc. . . ."

"Yankees can't fight, etc. . . ."

"Our Revolutionary fathers succeeded. Ergo, we are certain in like manner to succeed, etc. . . ."

"We can't be subjugated, etc. . . ."

"Slavery is right—our cause is righteous and a righteous God is bound to guarantee our ultimate success, etc."[62]

After the war, Lyon stayed on in the Columbus church—incurring some difficulties with his congregation over Reconstruction and salary—until 1870, when he resigned to become professor of metaphysics, logic, and political science at the University of Mississippi. At the General Assembly of 1870, he worked diligently, though unsuccessfully, to reunite southern and northern Presbyterians.[63]

Such is a partial and possibly representative account of those dissenting clergy in the old South during the antebellum and war years of the mid-nineteenth century. After the war, a Methodist newspaper declared that most ministerial disapproval of the South's actions manifested itself only in silence.[64] Those who chose to voice their disapproval of slavery, secession, and war were a small exception among their fellow clergy. By the beginning of 1861, dissent had been radically reduced in the South. When the war began a few months later, only a very few dissenters remained who dared to speak their convictions. Such a reduction in dissent continued until the summer of 1863 that brought with it the twin Confederate defeats at Vicksburg and Gettysburg. Then, when it became more and more apparent that the Confederate cause was a "lost cause," dissensions began to increase. Membership in the various peace societies increased, the desertion rate from the Confederate military became a problem of colossal proportions, and a few clergy members, who had previously held their peace on secession and war, began to voice mild objections. From July 1863 to the end of the war, the dissenters became a growing minority, but it is important to remember that they were always a small minority.

Four

Conclusion: The Creative Minority

THERE ARE SIGNIFICANT insights to be gained by observing these dissenting ministers in the old South in the years from 1830 to 1865. The first is that the South, even in the war years, was never a monolithic society. During the winnowing years of 1830 to 1861, when enormous social pressures were exerted upon the southern populace to speak with one voice in proclaiming the virtues of slavery, there were nonconforming voices who spoke and wrote boldly in denouncing the institution as unjust, un-American, and ungodly. When the war began in April 1861, though the unity in the South was significant and remarkable, there were still those who risked being labeled as traitors, with all the unpleasant consequences that such a label could entail, and spoke out against secession and the resulting war. Many of these dissenting voices during the war belonged to those who loved the South and considered themselves to be southern patriots but who also believed that secession and war were the surest way to destroy the cherished southern way of life. James Lyon, it will be recalled, was to be found in this category. He noted that "this cruel war has at last ended by the complete subjugation of the South." Lyon did not blame the North for the humiliation but rather placed blame upon southern "demagogues who had subjected and enslaved the people" with "lies of the basest kind." The war brought great havoc and suffering to countless numbers in the Confederacy. As the struggle came to an end, the dissenters were not happy over the tragic state of affairs, but as one said, whatever happened, it would be "a plaguery sight better than we're doing now."[1]

Those few dissenters proved to be right in their prophecies that secession and war would bring an end to a cherished way of life. It is often so. Arnold Toynbee once proclaimed that the hope of every civilization is to be found in its "creative minority," the few who understand what the current challenges are and offer new answers to counter new problems. When, according to Toynbee, the voices of the creative minority are so stifled that they are no longer heard or heeded in the land, then that civilization is ready to join others from the past on the ash heap of history. Though there may be some problems with such a theory, there is truth enough for people of all time and in every place to heed. Toynbee has written that the "creative personalities" must be able to carry others in a society, but should not expect to do it quickly.

> Those creative personalities who set a civilization in motion and carry it forward . . . cannot go on moving forward themselves unless they can contrive to carry their fellows with them in their advance; and the uncreative rank-and-file of Mankind, which in every known society has always been in an overwhelming majority, cannot be transformed *en masse* in the twinkling of an eye."[2]

The old South did not heed the voices of its dissenters, its creative minority, and paid the consequences. Though dissident voices were fairly strong in such states as Tennessee, Virginia, and North Carolina, they also existed, though to a lesser degree, in states of the deep South such as Mississippi, Georgia, and Texas. In spite of intimidating efforts by society, the courts, the military, and vigilante groups to enforce unanimity, there were still a few courageous people who would not conform. South Carolina appears to have been the most successful state when it came to stifling dissent. It is very difficult for the researcher to uncover such voices in that state. Remember, by the time the war began, a moderate and sympathetic voice like that of Richard Fuller had been gone from the state for fourteen years. Nevertheless, even in the state that led all others in seceding from the Union, there were always a few voices of dissent. As the war neared its end, some South Carolinians began to find their way into the secretive peace societies.

The fact that the dissenting clergy were so few in number supports the thesis that the clergy are more reflectors of society than molders. Richard E. Beringer and his coauthors, after noting the influence of the southern clergy upon the populace in the prewar and Civil War South, added an important word of caution about that influence: "But one should not presume that the clergy controlled or that they duped the people; if anything, they reflected rather than molded public opinion."[3] In the old South, the great majority of the clergy mirrored the dominant cultural point of view, and the few clerical dissenters reflected the small minority of dissenters in the public at large.[4] The same observation can be made about the northern clergy. The slow acceptance of abolitionism in the North is mirrored in the utterances and writings of most of the northern ministers. Theodore Parker, the outspoken Unitarian minister from Boston who was a leader in formulating antislavery sentiment in New England, was impatient with his fellow northern ministers for their failure to take a bold and forthright stand against slavery. He accused them of being reflectors of current opinion rather than shapers. "Once the clergy were the masters of the people," he affirmed, "and the authors of public opinion to a great degree; now they are chiefly the servants of the people, and but seldom aspire to lead it, except in the matters of their own craft, such as the technicalities of a sect, or the form of a ritual."[5]

For most clerics, it would seem, the vital role they play in regard to public opinion is that they reinforce beliefs that are currently and popularly held by giving them divine sanction. As an example, one can trace the development of northern thought and opinions on slavery by observing the evolution of Henry Ward Beecher's sermons on the subject. A Beecher biographer, Paxton Hibben, has written that Beecher, the most popular preacher in America in the mid–nineteenth century, was "a barometer and record" of what was happening in society. "He was not in advance of his day," wrote Hibben, "but precisely abreast of his day—the drum major's part in more than one sense."[6] A similar observation could be made about many, probably most, preachers. It would be difficult for a minister to survive in his or her vocation if that minister did not share to a large degree the values and sentiments of the constituency. Nevertheless, in every age and place, there have always been a small number of clergy, a bold minority, who have dared to confront, accuse, defy, and challenge the dominant values, beliefs, and practices of their societies. Theodore Parker in the North and the southern dissenters mentioned throughout this work were a part of this bold minority. Such people have usually paid a dear price for their nonconformity; yet, in the long-term perspective, they are often the people that history later venerates.

Because most ministers are reflectors of culture, the sermons they deliver are important historical documents, documents that are often overlooked by historians. As mirrors of current thought, the preachers of sermons throughout American history have become popular by reflecting the opinions, hopes, fears, prejudices, likes, and dislikes of a significant number of people. To read an adequate sample of sermons stemming from a certain time and place is an important step in grasping the essence of that society and culture. This is especially true of the Civil War era, a time when religion was of great importance on the American scene. Students of the sectional crisis have tended to neglect nineteenth-century sermons because of a perception that they are heavily theological, difficult to understand, and not as relevant as other types of historical documents. Although some sermons from this era fit this description, many others, as observed in the introduction of this work, are highly political, deeply passionate about various social issues, and examples of powerful and beautiful rhetoric. Through these sermons—and there are hundreds of them available—the researcher gains a greater insight into the passions, arguments, and biases that culminated in the war when Americans took up arms against each other.[7]

Some of these dissenting clergy espoused their views with the support and affirmation of others. James Lyon was supported by a congregation upon whom pressures were exerted to turn against him. In east Tennessee, there was a large constituency of Unionists, religious and secular, who worked together to oppose secession and the war efforts of the Confederacy. The Reverend William B. Carter worked with a network of others in the burning of bridges and other acts of sabotage. For the most part, however, dissenters were distressingly isolated from others. As has been discussed, even those who agreed or sympathized with the dissenters, failed to befriend or support them for fear of guilt by association. Eugene D. Genovese has written that even "proslavery divines" hesitated to publish sermons that called "for more humane treatment of slaves" in fear that "even proslavery sermons might be misconstrued at moments of high political temperature. Few if any voices," notes Genovese, "rose to defend those who attacked slavery and then met violence."[8] If challenging slavery resulted in isolation, the challenging of secession and war brought even greater loneliness. The consequences for such "treason" were severe, so that most of those who opposed secession held their peace. Those few who spoke against it, especially in the deep South, became extremely lonely people.

When one searches for some common thread that connects these various dissenters, it would seem to be that each of them had certain exposures to and links with the North. This exposure to a dissimilar way of life and to a different point of view, more than any other single factor, led to dissenting opinions, words, and actions. This accounts for the fact that that there was more dissension in the upper South and border states than in the lower South. Those living in Virginia and Tennessee were much more likely to be exposed to northern people, ideas, and publications than were those living in South Carolina and Mississippi.

Not until Richard Fuller moved from South Carolina to Maryland did he began to understand and articulate that slavery "fosters indolence and luxury" and was "not a good thing." Fuller's fellow South Carolinian, William Henry Brisbane, changed from a proslavery to an antislavery stance only after he read the antislavery arguments of Francis Wayland from Brown University in Rhode Island. Solomon McKinney, "Parson" Blount, Anthony Bewley, and Wesley Smith all maintained affiliations with the northern portion of the Methodist Episcopal Church after the denominational schism of 1844. John H. Aughey was born and educated in the North. Daniel Worth, though born in North Carolina, spent his formative years in the North. John Gregg Fee, though born and raised in Kentucky, and though a member of a slaveowning family, was educated at two northern colleges before entering Lane Theological Seminary, where after an intense inner struggle, he was converted to abolitionism. Daniel Moncure Conway, born in Virginia to slaveholding parents, became an opponent of slavery because of the influences he encountered at Harvard University.

After the war began and the dissenting issue became primarily secession rather than slavery, it was still northern connections that seemed to contribute most heavily to Unionism in the South. Though William G. Brownlow was always a Union man, it was not until he spent some time in the North, due to his ouster from Tennessee, that he put aside his deeply held proslavery views and came out in favor of emancipation. Marble Nash Taylor was accused of fraternizing with Yankees. The strong antislavery views of Eli Washington Caruthers were formulated at Princeton

University. James Sinclair come to the South after his early and formative years had been spent elsewhere. Melinda Rankin came to Brownsville, Texas, from New England.

The Presbyterian denomination appeared to be disproportionately represented among the southern clergy dissenters. Robert J. Breckinridge from Kentucky; J. R. Graves from North Carolina; Melinda Rankin and Thaddedus McRae from Texas; and Galladet, John H. Aughey, James Pelan, and James Lyon from Mississippi were all Presbyterians. One of the reasons for the overrepresentation of Presbyterians among the dissenters was that out of the three largest Protestant denominations in the South (Methodists, Baptists, Presbyterians), only the Presbyterians had not suffered a formal sectional division before the war began. The southern Methodists and the Baptists had officially severed connections with their northern associates some fifteen years before the war. Presbyterian ministers in the South continued to have fellowship and communicate with their northern counterparts long after southern Methodists and Baptists had ceased to do so. Exposure to the North was broadened even further by the fact that many southern Presbyterian ministers had been born in the North and/or were educated there. "Here then," comments John K. Bettersworth, "was a church that had preserved much of its national character to the end. It also seems to have possessed a degree of open-mindedness on the whole questions of slavery and secession because of the fact that it was essentially the church of the educated, liberally inclined urban communities."[9]

How was it that a few, a very few, dissenting clergy members were able to hold on to their positions in the years before and during the war, while most of their fellow dissenters were either banished from the South, dismissed from their churches, driven to financial ruin, imprisoned, or executed? There would appear to be no single reason that covers all. Circumstances, personal and societal, varied from one individual to another. Robert J. Breckinridge in Kentucky was able to maintain prominent positions in the state before and during the war in spite of strong verbal and written attacks upon the institution of slavery. The record indicates that he was able to do so because of the prominence and importance of his family. His fellow Kentuckian, John Gregg Fee, lacked such prominent family connections and was forced out of the state.

In Virginia, the Quaker minister, Samuel McPherson Janney, strongly denounced slavery before the war. Though he was twice indicted in the summer of 1850 for published articles that attacked slavery, he escaped conviction both times. When the war commenced, Janney stayed on in Virginia where he continued his attacks upon slavery and supported the Union. While others who expressed similar views were forced to leave the state or were imprisoned, Janney was able to remain in the state without compromising or stifling his convictions. The reason that Janney was able to do so apparently lay within his own Quaker personality. He was tactful, intelligent, articulate, and displayed a character that was beyond reproach. The fact that during the war he cared for the wounded of both the northern and southern armies demonstrated to all that his compassion crossed both racial and sectional lines.

Breckinridge and Janney were both from the upper South where if a dissenter had any possibility of surviving, it would be in such states. But how was it that James A. Lyon from Mississippi was able to hold his pastorate when his staunch Unionism was so objectionable to most citizens in the state. In Mississippi, dissenters such as James Phelan were killed, and John H. Aughey would have been had he not escaped from prison. Lyon, on the other hand, not only avoided banishment, imprisonment, or death, he actually held a position of pastoral leadership, prominence, and respect throughout the war, though he encountered some difficulties. Part of the answer for Lyon's success is to be found in the character and accomplishments of Lyon himself. He had served the First Presbyterian Church in Columbus, Mississippi, since 1841 with the exception of a seven years' absence due to health reasons.[10] Over that time, he had built up the church and had established a most favorable reputation among his parishioners, the community, and the Presbyterian denomination. The fact that Lyon was himself a slaveholder undoubtedly did much to identify him with the southern way of life. His congregation and others understood that Lyon opposed secession not because he wanted to destroy a particular lifestyle but because he wanted to preserve it.

It should come as no surprise that some of these dissenting clergy met with such violence. Though Americans, perhaps especially southern Americans, were, at this point in history, deeply religious and pious, history teaches that piety is no insurance against violence. Some of the most bitter, cruel, and violent wars ever fought have been religious in nature. As was noted in the introduction, this was especially true of America's Civil War. Sidney E. Ahlstrom has written of the preaching throughout the nation during the war: "The pulpits resounded with a vehemence and absence of restraint never equaled in American history." Beringer and his colleagues have noted that "at no time was organized religion in the United States more active politically than in the twenty years prior to the war," and, therefore, they assert that in a real sense "the war was one between the churches of the North and those of the South."[11] If the clergy and the churches played such leading roles in the sectional strife, it is little wonder that dissident clergy were looked upon, on both sides of the Mason-Dixon Line, as the ultimate traitors and thus became the recipients of harsh reprisals. When each side believed that its cause was God's cause, there was little room and not much desire for compromise and amicable solutions. Cultural tunnel vision and ardent nationalism mixed with religious passion became a recipe for intolerance and violence.

This study is also a commentary on a mindset that existed and was, in some places and under certain circumstances, encouraged within the Confederacy. Though the

Confederacy formally declared its commitment to democracy and liberty, it harbored and often protected many citizens who were eager to crush dissent by whatever means. As has been noted, the suffocating of dissent was sometimes carried out through legally supported means and, at other times, by those, such as vigilante groups, who operated outside of, yet, with the approval of, the legal system.

Problems for dissenters in the South did not end with the culmination of the war. It will be recalled that the Reverend James Sinclair—a slaveowning Unionist from North Carolina—testified before Congress early in 1866 that he thought it too dangerous for him to return to the state. "I know," he asserted, "it is utterly impossible for any man who was not true to the Confederate States up to the last moment of the existence of the confederacy, to expect any favor of these people as the State is constituted at present."[12]

An incident that supports the concept that the South, or some portions of it at least, was not ready to tolerate dissent even at the war's end, happened in Newnan, Georgia, in June 1865. The Reverend John H. Caldwell, pastor of the Methodist church in Newnan, had been a slaveowner and an ardent defender of the Confederacy throughout the war. On January 18, 1865, the citizens of Newnan gathered at Caldwell's church to declare their continued loyalty to a nearly defeated Confederacy and to express their displeasure with certain citizens in Savannah who had agreed to submit to the United States government, whose troops occupied that city. A committee was appointed to draft resolutions. Caldwell was selected to be the chairman of the committee and then became the author of the resolutions that renewed "our vows of loyalty" and rebuked "the spirit and conduct of the ignoble few" in Savannah who were deserving of "unqualified scorn and contempt."

Five months later, Caldwell switched sides and himself became the recipient of "unqualified scorn and contempt." On Sunday, June 4, on his forty-fifth birthday, and only a few days after the last Confederate military defeat, Caldwell personally wrestled within himself as to the meaning of the war and the place of slavery. After a night of inner struggle, he came to the conclusion that slavery was the chief cause of the war and the destruction of the institution was a great good. He purposed within himself to preach to his congregation on "a long forbidden topic— the evils of slavery." On the following Sunday, June 11, Caldwell delivered a sermon, "Abuses of Slavery," to a congregation completely unaware of the radical change in their pastor's stance. In the sermon, the pastor charged that the Confederacy had been defeated because it was morally wrong on the issue of slavery. "If our practice had been conformed to the law of God," declared Caldwell, "he would not have suffered the institution to be overthrown." Before the sermon was over, at least one-third of the congregation had walked out, "among them," said Caldwell, "some of my best friends and some of the wealthiest and most influential members and supporters of the church."

The next Sunday, Caldwell returned to his unexpected theme of the prior week. In this sermon, he emphasized that historical truth had been denied to most of the southern population. Caldwell said he showed his congregation a history they "never knew before," because no one had told them. Their ministers had not told them because the clergy were either ignorant of the truth themselves, or knowing it, would not reveal it. "We have sinned," exclaimed Caldwell, "and God has smitten us." The devastation and destruction of the South was "what our Church and ministry have done to bring all this ruin upon us."

After this second sermon, an angry congregation appealed to the presiding elder of the LaGrange District, who removed Caldwell from the Newnan church and reassigned him to a remote area of the district. Caldwell appealed the decision to Bishop George F. Pierce, who would not listen to the appeal. The deposed minister then appealed to Major General George H. Thomas, the Union commander of the Division of Tennessee. Thomas reinstated Caldwell to his pastorate in Newnan and commanded local Federal forces to protect him.[13]

Until well into the twentieth century, dissent, especially in matters pertaining to race, was a harrowing stance in many of the states of the old Confederacy. Ministers who challenged the morality of segregation and worked for social justice in equal treatment of the races found themselves dismissed from their churches, intimidated both verbally and physically, shunned, and made to understand the importance and necessity of conformity to dominant and prevailing views and values. As in the old South, through the ensuing decades, there were many among the southern clergy who held grave personal reservations about the morality of racial discrimination and segregation, but, who, in order to protect themselves and their families from social abuses, as well as a desire to preserve their vocations, maintained a policy of silence. After all, they reasoned, one cannot have a ministry if there is no congregation to whom one can minister.

An example of twentieth-century dissent, of one who did not adopt a stance of silence about or blindness to racial ills, was Clarence Jordan (1912–1969), a Baptist minister and the founder of Koinonia Farm not far from Americus, Georgia. Jordan, who is probably most remembered for his "Cottonpatch" translations of the New Testament, established in 1942, along with others, an interracial farming cooperative. In the midst of an area where segregation had placed African Americans on the lowest rungs of the socioeconomic ladder, Koinonia Farm was designed to be a model of integration and racial equality. Jordan's thoughts on racial justice had formed early in his life. During his Sunday school days, he had learned a song which went,

> Red and yellow, black and white,
> They are precious in his sight;
> Jesus loves the little children of the world.

In his personal journal, Jordan recorded the thoughts that were stimulated by this song.

> The question arose in my mind, "Were the little black children precious in God's sight just like the little white children?" The song said they were. Then why were they always so ragged, so dirty and hungry? Did God have favorite children?
>
> I could not figure out the answers to these puzzling questions, but I knew something was wrong. A little light came when I came to realize that perhaps it wasn't God's doings, but man's. God didn't turn them away from our churches—we did. God didn't pay them low wages—we did. God didn't make them live in another section of town and in miserable huts—we did. God didn't make ragged, hungry little boys pick rotten oranges and fruit out of the garbage can and eat them— we did. Maybe they were just as precious in God's sight, but were they in ours? My environment told me that they were not very precious in anybody's sight. A nigger was a nigger and must be kept in his place—the place of servitude and inferiority.[14]

Jordan's social experiment had been in operation only a few days when Koinonia Farm was visited by representatives of the Ku Klux Klan. The spokesman of the group said to Jordan: "We understand you been taking your meals with the nigger." Softly, Jordan replied, "Well, now, at lunchtime we usually eat with a man we've hired." To this the Klansman retorted: "We're from the Ku Klux Klan, and we're here to tell you we don't allow the sun to set on anybody who eats with niggers." Over the next several years, especially during the 1950s and early 1960s, the hostility toward Jordan and his interracial farm increased dramatically. The cooperative farming venture became the target of bombs, vandalism, shootings, and boycotts. A store that did business with Koinonia Farm was bombed. Fortunately, no one was ever killed, though fired bullets came within inches of some who were living on and working at the farm. Appeals to local law enforcement agencies went unheeded. Even an appeal to President Eisenhower brought no help or protection. A Georgia grand jury charged that Koinonia Farm was a communist front.[15]

Most disappointing of all was the failure of any local churches to stand by this Christian experiment. Clarence Jordan, his family, and some others at the farm were dismissed from membership at the local Baptist Church because of the dissident group's stance on integration. At a local Klan rally, a minister called for "all red-blooded Americans who are proud of their white race" to uphold the biblical teachings on segregation. In a speech, after referring to the various persecutions that Koinonia Farm had experienced, Jordan spoke of the compliance and acquiescence of many Christians in the terror. "I would rather," he declared, "face the frantic, childish mob, even with their shotguns and buggy whips, than the silent, insidious mob of good church people who give assent to boycott and subtle psychological warfare. What can I say for those who know the word of God and will not speak it?" As to why many people could not or would not live out the principles of their faith, Jordan responded, "The answer is fear." The farmer-preacher-biblical scholar thundered: "Faith and fear, like light and darkness, are incompatible. Fear is the polio of the soul, which prevents our walking by faith."[16]

Dissidents, at any time or any place, have always found their lot to be a difficult one. Society seldom appreciates its nonconformists, whether they are named Socrates, Thoreau, Aughey, or Jordan. Yet in the long run of history, many of these dissidents have proved to be more accurate in their assessments than the majority who hold the dissidents in such great disdain. Slavery—once championed by a majority, but denounced by a few such as Daniel Worth or John G. Fee—has disappeared from American society and no moral person today would wish its return. The breakup of the Union—once the dominant desire of those in the old South, although opposed by a minority that included Charles Gillette and James A. Lyon—is no longer an option for any state for any reason. Segregation—once the accepted and legal way of life in parts of the South to well into the twentieth century, though battled by a lonely few such as Clarence Jordan—is no longer legally sanctioned. Dissidents are not always right. Their numbers sometime include the demented and the demagogues, the deranged and the dense. However, such labels must not be too hastily applied, for dissidents may also be the "creative minority," those few in whom the hope of the future resides.

Notes

Bibliography

Index

Notes

1. The Stance of the Majority

1. James W. Silver, *Confederate Morale and Church Propaganda* (New York: Norton, 1957), 93, 101; Mitchell Snay, *Gospel of Disunion: Religion and Separatism in the Antebellum South* (Cambridge: Cambridge University Press, 1993), 5, 11; Emory M. Thomas, *The Confederate Nation, 1861–1865* (New York: HarperCollins, 1979), 21; Willard E. Wight, "The Churches and the Confederate Cause," *Civil War History* 6 (1960): 373; H. Sheldon Smith, *In His Image, but . . . Racism in Southern Religion* (Durham, NC: Duke University Press, 1972), 188.

2. For one contemporary observation, see *The Knoxville Whig*, 18 May 1861; William G. Brownlow, *Sketches of the Rise, Progress, and Decline of Secession* (Philadelphia: George Childs, 1862), 111–12; Robert Livingston Stanton, *The Church and the Rebellion: A Consideration of the Rebellion Against the Government of the United States; and the Agency of the Church, North and South, in Relation Thereto* (New York: Derby & Miller, 1864), vi.

3. C. C. Goen, *Broken Churches, Broken Nation* (Macon, GA: Mercer University Press, 1985), 6, 13, 67. Goen's book may be the best single source on the denominational schisms, their meanings, and implications.

4. William Warren Sweet, *The Story of Religion in America* (New York: Harper, 1950), 312; Allen Nevins, *Ordeal of the Union* (New York: Scribner's, 1947), 2:553; Charles S. Sydnor, *The Development of Southern Sectionalism, 1819–1848* (Baton Rouge: Louisiana State University Press, 1934), 299–300.

5. William A. Booth, *The Writings of William A. Booth, M.D. During the Controversy upon Slavery* (Somerville, TN: Reeves and Yancy, 1845), 6; *Alabama Baptist*, Dec. 6, 1845, in Snay, *Gospel of Disunion*, 139–40. *Minutes of the State Convention of the Baptist Denomination in South Carolina, at its Twenty-Fourth Anniversary, held at Darlington Baptist Church, commencing on the 7th, and ending on the 10th of December* (n.p., n.d.), 7.

6. Calhoun and Clay are quoted in Goen, *Broken Churches, Broken Nation*, 104–6.

7. Silver, *Confederate Morale and Church Propaganda*, 17, 18–19.

8. All quotes found in Snay, *Gospel of Disunion*, 154, 155, 152.

9. Anne C. Loveland, *Southern Evangelicals and the Social Order, 1800–1860* (Baton Rouge: Louisiana State University Press, 1980), 191.

10. Eugene D. Genovese, *The Slaveholders' Dilemma: Freedom and Progress in Southern Conservative Thought, 1820–1860* (Columbia, SC: University of South Carolina Press, 1992), 36.

11. Donald G. Matthews, *Religion in the Old South* (Chicago: University of Chicago Press, 1977), 157.

12. *Liberator*, Jan. 1, 1931; Sydney E. Ahlstrom, *A Religious History of the American People* (New Haven: Yale University Press, 1972), 652.

13. Joseph Tracey, *Natural Equality* (Windsor, VT: Chronicle Press, 1833); Simon Clough, *A Candid Appeal to the Citizens of the United States* (New York: A. K. Bertran, 1834); Horace Bushnell, *A Discourse on the Slavery Question* (Hartford, CT: Case Library, 1839); George Junkin, *The Integrity of Our National Union* (Cincinnati: R. P. Donogh, 1843); Charles Porter, *Our Country's Danger and Security* (Utica, NY: R. W. Roberts, 1844); Garrison quoted in John R. Bodo, *The Protestant Clergy and Public Issues, 1812–1848* (Princeton, NJ: Princeton University Press, 1954), 137.

14. Snay, *Gospel of Disunion*, 30, 32; Thornwell quoted in Genovese, *Slaveholders' Dilemma*, 31.

15. Theodore Clapp, *Slavery* (New Orleans: John Gibson, 1838); Samuel Dunwoody, *A Sermon on the Subject of Slavery* (Columbia, SC: S. Weir, 1837); W. T. Hamilton, *Duties of Masters and Slaves Respectively; or, Domestic Slavery as Sanctioned by the Bible* (Mobile, AL: F. H. Brooks, 1844).

16. Donald Matthews (*Religion in the Old South*, 171) has summarized this "imaginative" biblical interpretation:

> If one were really imaginative, he could find the origins of black people in the unnatural coupling of the accursed and exiled Cain with a female from among "pre-Adamites," who had been created before humanity. For the more traditional bibliophile, there was a sufficient

explanation in the curse of the drunken Noah upon the descendants of his son, Ham (Africans), because of an invasion of the patriarch's privacy. And a few expositors argued—just to complete the circle no doubt—that Ham had actually married into the race of Cain, thus making blacks twice cursed. That anyone was converted by such explanations is doubtful, for they were merely a way of lending legitimacy to views already shaped by personal experience, psychic need, and social interaction.

17. Richard Fuller and Francis Wayland, *Domestic Slavery Considered as a Scriptural Institution* (New York: Lewis Colby, 1845), 147–48.

18. Loveland, *Southern Evangelicals and the Social Order*, 201–2.

19. Matthews, *Religion in the Old South*, 169–70.

20. *Religion in the Old South*, 170; Frederick A. Ross, *Slavery Ordained of God* (Philadelphia: J. B. Lippincott & Co., 1859), 55–58, 124–25.

21. Josiah Priest, *Bible Defense of Slavery: and Origin, Fortunes and History of the Negro Race* (Glasgow, KY: W. S. Brown, M.D., 1852), 228–29.

22. James Henley Thornwell, *The Rights and the Duties of Masters* (Charleston, SC: Walker and James, 1850).

23. Isaac T. Tichenor, *Fast Day Sermon* (Montgomery, AL: Montgomery Advertiser Book and Job Printing Office, 1863); southern journal quoted in Loveland, *Southern Evangelicals and the Social Order*, 259–60; Snay, *Gospel of Disunion*, 75, 77.

24. William O. Prentiss, *A Sermon Preached at St. Peter's Church, Charleston, by the Rev. William O. Prentiss, on Wednesday, November 21, 1860, being a Day of Public Fasting, Humiliation and Prayer* (Charleston, SC: Evans & Cogswell, 1860), 15; Andrew H. H. Boyd, *Thanksgiving Sermon, delivered in Winchester, Virginia, on Thursday, 29th November, 1860* (Winchester: Winchester Virginian, 1860), 12; Edwin T. Winkler, *Duties of the Christian Soldier* (Charleston, SC: A. J. Burke, 1861); George Foster Pierce, *Sermon* (Milledgeville, GA: Groughton, Nisbet, and Barnes, 1863).

25. Prentiss, *A Sermon*, 17; H. N. Pierce, *Sermon Preached in St. John's Church, Mobile, on the 13th of June, 1861, the National Fast Appointed by His Excellency Jefferson Davis, President of the Confederate States of America* (Mobile, AL: Farrow & Dennett,

1861), 12; the resolution can be found in W. Harrison Daniel, "The Southern Baptists in the Confederacy," *Civil War History* 6 (1960): 389–90.

26. *Southern Presbyterian*, Mar. 9, 1861; Thomas Atkinson, *On the Causes of our National Troubles. A Sermon delivered in St. James Church, Wilmington, N.C. on Friday, the 4th of January, 1861* (Wilmington, NC: Herald Book and Job Office, 1861), 6; William B. McCash, *Thomas R. R. Cobb (1823–1862): The Making of a Southern Nationalist* (Macon, GA: Mercer University Press, 1983), 89.

27. Excerpt from the *Southern Presbyterian*, as quoted in Snay, *Gospel of Disunion*, 173; *Proceedings of the Southern Baptist Convention, May 10–13, 1861* (Richmond: MacFarlane and Fergusson, 1861), 63; Joseph Stiles, *National Rectitude the Only True Basis of National Prosperity: An Appeal to the Confederate States* (Petersburg, VA: Evangelical Tract Society, 1863).

28. Joseph R. Wilson, *Mutual Relations of Masters and Slaves as Taught in the Bible* (Augusta, GA: Steam Power Press of Chronicle and Sentinel, 1861); quoted in Jack P. Maddox, Jr., "Proslavery Millennialism: Social Eschatology in Antebellum Southern Calvinism," *American Quarterly* 31 (spring 1979): 58.

29. Silver, *Confederate Morale and Church Propaganda*, 16–17.

30. Margaret B. DesChamps, "Benjamin Morgan Palmer, Orator-Preacher of the Confederacy," *Southern Speech Journal* 19 (Sept. 1953): 16. This article is a brief but excellent account of Palmer's activities during the war. The quote from Reverend Hoge is found in Ernest Trice Thompson, *Presbyterianism in the South*, vol. 1, *1607–1861* (Richmond, VA: John Knox Press, 1963), 553. Snay, *Gospel of Disunion*, 151.

31. Benjamin Morgan Palmer, "Slavery a Divine Trust: Duty of the South to Preserve and Perpetuate It," in *Fast Day Sermons*, 60, 61, 62, 65–66, 68, 70, 71–72, 77.

32. Loveland, *Southern Evangelicals and the Social Order*, 192.

33. Baptist assoc. quoted in Richmond *Enquirer*, Sept. 29, 1835; *Southern Baptist and General Intelligencer*, Oct. 9, 1835; Carl N. Degler, *The Other South: Southern Dissenters in the Nineteenth Century* (New York: Harper & Row, 1974), 78; Snay, *Gospel of Disunion*, 36.

34. Richard E. Beringer et al., *Why the South Lost the Civil War* (Athens: University of Georgia Press, 1986), 97.

35. Robert Lewis Dabney, *The Christian's Best Motive for Patriotism* (Richmond, VA: Chas. H. Wynn, 1860), 4, 8; the Jan.

1861 remarks in Thomas C. Johnson, *The Life and Letters of Robert Lewis Dabney* (1903; reprint, Edinburgh: Banner of Truth Trust, 1977), 198–210, 222–23. Dabney, at an earlier time in his career, had found severe weaknesses in the institution of slavery, an example being that the female slave was not the mistress of her chastity. He would later change his mind and defend slavery based upon his understanding of the teachings of the Bible. As it was with so many others, it was the abolitionists who played a large part in the change of Dabney's position on slavery. Dabney regarded the abolitionists as infidels who contributed much to southern intransigence. See Clement Eaton, *Freedom of Thought in the Old South* (Durham, NC: Duke University Press, 1940), 276–77.

36. Benjamin Morgan Palmer, *The Life and Letters of James Henley Thornwell* (Richmond, VA: Whittet & Shepperson, 1875), 477–78; James Henley Thornwell, "Critical Notices," *Southern Presbyterian Review* 4 (Jan. 1861): 452.

37. James Henley Thornwell, "Our National Sins," in *Fast Day Sermons*, 56; letter from Thornwell found in Palmer, *Life and Letters of Thornwell*, 486; Thornwell's article quoted in Silver, *Confederate Morale and Church Propaganda*, 16–17; Loveland, *Southern Evangelicals and the Social Order*, 258. Eugene D. Genovese has placed both James Henley Thornwell and Robert L. Dabney among the great intellectuals of the old South. They belong in the class, claims Genovese, with other great southern intellectuals such as St. George Tucker, T. R. R. Cobb, Thomas Ruffin, George Tucker, Jacob N. Cardozo, Thomas Roderick Dew, William H. Trescott, John C. Calhoun, and Albert Taylor Bledsoe; all men who "deserve to rank among America's ablest thinkers." These and other southern intellectuals were men of great ability and influence, Genovese contends, but because they were on the losing side, "the southern intellectuals have virtually been expunged from memory." *Slaveholders' Dilemma*, 2, 3.

38. James M. McPherson, *Battle Cry of Freedom: The Civil War Era* (New York: Oxford University Press, 1988), 213.

39. Eaton, *Freedom of Thought in the Old South*, ix, 292, vii, 296, 314.

40. Quoted in Silver, *Confederate Morale and Church Propaganda*, 75.

41. Thomas Dunaway, *A Sermon* (Richmond, VA: Enquirer Book and Job Press, 1864).

42. Benjamin Morgan Palmer, *A Discourse Before the General*

Assembly of South Carolina (Columbia, SC: Charles P. Pelham, State Printers, 1864), Beringer et al., *Why the South Lost the Civil War*, 101.

43. Drew Gilpin Faust, *The Creation of Confederate Nationalism: Ideology and Identity in the Civil War South* (Baton Rouge: Louisiana State University Press, 1988), 22, 26, 29.

44. John Paris, *Funeral Discourse* (Greensborough, NC: A. W. Ingold & Co., 1864).

2. The Winnowing Years, 1830–1861

1. Fuller and Wayland, *Domestic Slavery Considered as a Scriptural Institution*, 170, 188, 200. Fuller was a man whose disposition was so constituted that he could debate without rancor. In 1839, he and his friend, John England, the Catholic bishop of Charleston, became involved in a protracted debate over prohibition, which was published in the *Charleston Courier* (July 1839–Sept. 1839). Though the debate was conducted with strong feelings and deep convictions, it was also marked by great personal courtesy on both sides.

2. Richard Fuller, *Address Before the American Colonization Society* (Baltimore: Office of the Trust Union, 1851).

3. The information on W. H. Brisbane is taken from Larry E. Tise, *Proslavery: A History of the Defense of Slavery in America, 1701–1840* (Athens: University of Georgia Press, 1987), 313–16; 422–23 n. 3.

4. Wesley Norton, "The Methodist Episcopal Church and the Civil Disturbances in North Texas in 1859 and 1860," *Southwestern Historical Quarterly* 68 (Jan. 1965): 329.

5. For accounts of the Bewley incident, see Norton, "The Methodist Episcopal Church and the Civil Disturbances in North Texas," 331–41; Walter P. Webb et al., eds., *The Handbook of Texas* (Austin: Texas State Historical Assoc., 1952), 1:153–54; and James Marten, *Texas Divided: Loyalty and Dissent in the Lone Star State, 1856–1874* (Lexington: University Press of Kentucky, 1990), 6–8.

6. Charles Elliott, *South-western Methodism: A History of the Methodist Episcopal Church in the South-West from 1844 to 1864*, ed. LeRoy M. Vernon (Cincinnati: Poe & Hitchcock, 1868), 163–65. Tom Willett was Bewley's son-in-law and coworker in

the ministry. He was never taken captive. Though Elliott's work is a polemic against the Confederacy, slavery, secession, and the Methodist Episcopal Church, South, it does contain several factual accounts of what it meant to oppose the Confederate ideology, mostly in Missouri, but to some extent in Texas.

7. Silver, *Confederate Morale and Church Propaganda*, 20; Marten, *Texas Divided*, 11.

8. Marten, *Texas Divided*, 11, 8. For an excellent article dealing with the subject of mob violence throughout the South during those passionate times, see Clement Eaton, "Mob Violence in the Old South," *Mississippi Valley Historical Review* 29 (Dec. 1942): 351–70.

9. Hinton Rowan Helper, *The Impending Crisis of the South: How to Meet It* (New York: A. B. Burdick, 1860). Though Helper called himself an "immediate abolitionist," what he really wanted was the colonization of the liberated slaves. Helper held deep prejudices against African Americans. Once he refused to eat in a restaurant that employed black waiters and would write a book, *The Negroes in Negroland*, which bitterly attacked those of the black race. See Eaton, *Freedom of Thought in the Old South*, 223.

10. Degler, *The Other South*, 88; Worth's letter recorded in Noble J. Tolbert, "Daniel Worth: Tar Heel Abolitionist," *North Carolina Historical Review* 39 (summer 1962): 290.

11. Degler, *The Other South*, 89; *North Carolina Presbyterian*, Nov. 26, 1859; quotes from other religious publications in Tolbert, "Daniel Worth," 291, 292; jail cell described in Roy S. Nicholson, *Wesleyan Methodism in the South* (Syracuse, NY: Wesleyan Methodist Publishing House, 1933), 92–93.

12. The newspaper account is quoted in Tolbert, "Daniel Worth," 293.

13. "Daniel Worth," 297.

14. "Daniel Worth," 294 n. 40; account of trials in Nicholson, *Wesleyan Methodism in the South*, 97, 95.

15. Joseph Clarke Robert, *The Road to Monticello: A Study of the Virginia Slavery Debate of 1832* (Durham, NC: Duke University Press, 1941), v, 53.

16. John Hersey, *Appeal to Christians on the Subject of Slavery*, 3d ed. (Baltimore: Sherwood and Co., n.d.), 55–56, 86–88, v–xi. For further information on John Hersey, see F. E. Marine, *Sketch of Reverend John Hersey, Minister of the Gospel of the M.E. Church* (Baltimore: Hoffman & Co., 1879); and Patricia P. Hickin,

"Antislavery in Virginia, 1831–1861" (Ph.D. diss., University of Virginia, 1968), 374–81.

17. Account of Paxton's banishment in Eaton, *Freedom of Thought in the Old South*, 277; J. D. Paxton, *Letters on Slavery Addressed to the Cumberland Congregation, Virginia* (Lexington, KY: Abraham T. Skillman, 1833).

18. Eaton, *Freedom of Thought in the Old South*, 277; Wesley Smith, *A Defense of the Methodist Episcopal Church Against the Charges of Rev. S. Kelley and Others* (Fairmont, VA: Western Virginia Republican Office, 1855).

19. Degler, *The Other South*, 20–21, 24.

20. Breckinridge, "The Union to Be Preserved," in *Fast Day Sermons*, 100, 107, 109, 112–13, 119. See also Eaton, *Freedom of Thought in the Old South*, 276.

21. Eaton, 214–15; account of persecution in Edwin Rogers Embree, "A Kentucky Crusader," *American Mercury* 24 (Sept. 1931): 101, 102; the death of his opposition in John Gregg Fee, *Autobiography of John G. Fee, Berea, Kentucky* (Chicago: National Christian Assoc., 1891), 124.

22. Eaton, *Freedom of Thought in the Old South*, 215–16; account of sermon in Beecher's church and consequences in Fee, *Autobiography*, 146–47.

23. Embree, "A Kentucky Crusader," 98.

24. Conway, *Autobiography, Memories and Experiences of Moncure Daniel Conway* (Boston: Houghton Mifflin, 1904), 2:188.

25. Conway's visit to Falmouth is recorded in Eaton, *Freedom of Thought in the Old South*, 273–74.

26. Conway, *Autobiography*, 1:239, 240.

27. *Autobiography*, 1:242.

3. The War Years, 1861–1865

1. George C. Smith, *The Life and Letters of James Osgood Andrew, Bishop of the Methodist Episcopal Church, South* (Nashville: Southern Methodist Publishing House, 1883), 439; letter from Robert Topp can be found in Oliver P. Temple, *East Tennessee and the Civil War* (Cincinnati: Robert Clarke Co., 1899), 416; Wight, "The Churches and the Confederate Cause," 368–69; J. S. Hayes anecdote in W. Harrison Daniel, *Southern Protestantism in the Confederacy* (Bedford, VA: Print Shop, 1989), 46.

2. James Madison Pendleton, *Reminiscences of a Long Life* (Louisville, KY: Baptist Book Concern, 1891), 121, 122.

3. William G. Brownlow, *Helps to the Study of Presbyterianism or an Unsophisticated Exposition of Calvinism* (Knoxville: F. S. Heiskell Co., 1834); Brownlow, *The Great Iron Wheel Examined; or Its False Spokes Extracted* (Nashville: Brownlow, 1856), 203; quote on Baptists from Eaton, *Freedom of Thought in the Old South*, 291.

4. Eaton, *Freedom of Thought in the Old South*, 251; *Ought American Slavery to be Perpetuated? A Debate Between Rev. W. G. Brownlow and Rev. A. Pryne* (Philadelphia: J. P. Lippincott & Co., 1858), 270, 101, 33–34, 259–63.

5. Brownlow, *A Sermon on Slavery: A Vindication of the Methodist Church, South: Her Position Stated* (Knoxville, TN: Kinsloe & Rice, 1857); Brownlow's speech can be found in E. Merton Coulter, *William G. Brownlow: Fighting Parson of the Southern Highlands* (Chapel Hill: University of North Carolina Press, 1937), 130–31.

6. Coulter, *William G. Brownlow*, 137, 144.

7. *William G. Brownlow*, 191–2.

8. Noel Fisher, "'The Leniency Shown Them Has Been Unavailing': The Confederate Occupation of East Tennessee," *Civil War History* 40 (Dec. 1994): 280.

9. Haskel Monroe, "Southern Presbyterians and the Secession Crisis," *Civil War History* 6 (1960): 356.

10. Degler, *The Other South*, 27; Eaton, *Freedom of Thought in the Old South*, 238, 235. For a more detailed account of the Quaker migration from the South, see Stephen B. Weeks, *Southern Quakers and Slavery* (Baltimore: Johns Hopkins University Press, 1896).

11. Samuel H. Janney, *Memoirs* (Philadelphia: Friends Book Assoc., 1881), 100.

12. Eaton, *Freedom of Thought in the Old South*, 238.

13. Janney, *Memoirs*, 95, 93; Degler, *The Other South*, 36.

14. Janney, *Memoirs*, 97–98; Eaton, *Freedom of Thought in the Old South*, 136–37, 236.

15. Edward Needles Wright, *Conscientious Objectors in the Civil War* (1931; reprint, New York: A. S. Barnes & Co., 1961), 6; Lincoln to Eliza P. Gurney, Roy P. Basler, ed., *The Collected Works of Abraham Lincoln* (New Brunswick, NJ: Rutgers University Press, 1953), 7:535. For further information on the Quakers and the Civil War, see Peter Brock, "Quaker Conscientious

Objectors in the American Civil War," in *The Quaker Peace Testimony, 1660 to 1914* (York, Eng.: Sessions Book Trust, 1990), 166–83.

16. Wright, *Conscientious Objectors*, 4, 138,,172, 98, 205, 176–77.

17. *Conscientious Objectors*, 179.

18. Daniel, *Southern Protestantism in the Confederacy*, 43.

19. Wight, "The Churches and the Confederate Cause," 368; anecdote on Taylor in Joseph G. de Roulhac Hamilton, *Reconstruction in North Carolina* (1914; reprint, Freeport, NY: Books for Libraries Press, 1971), 84.

20. Frank L. Owsley, "Defeatism in the Confederacy," *North Carolina Historical Review* 3 (July 1926): 452, 454.

21. "Defeatism in the Confederacy," 453.

22. Georgia Lee Tatum, *Disloyalty in the Confederacy* (Chapel Hill: University of North Carolina Press, 1934), 130–31.

23. Eaton, *Freedom of Thought in the Old South*, 275; account of disapproved books in Eli Washington Caruthers, *The Life of David Caldwell* (Greensboro, NC: Swain & Sherwood, 1842), 263; information on manuscript from Degler, The Other South, 29.

24. As recorded in Degler, *The Other South*, 29–31.

25. Daniel, *Southern Protestantism in the Confederacy*, 43; information on Sinclair as recorded in Robert T. Marcus and Daniel Burner, *America Firsthand*, vol. 2, *From Reconstruction to the Present* (New York: St. Martin's Press, 1989), 23–28.

26. An account of Galladet's troubles are found in John H. Aughey, *Tupelo* (Lincoln, NE: State Journal Co., 1888), 71–72; the account of Mortimer's ostracism is in Daniel, *Southern Protestantism in the Confederacy*, 46.

27. Charles Gillette, *A Few Historic Records of the Church in the Diocese of Texas, During the Rebellion* (New York: John A. Gray & Green, 1865), 11–12; account of debate over prayer in Works Projects Administration (WPA), *St. David's Through the Years* (Austin: Betty Gilmer Chapter of St. David's Guild, 1942), 36.

28. The correspondence can be found in Gillette, *A Few Historic Records*. In the preface of his volume, Gillette stated his reasons for the book and the publication of the correspondence between himself and Gregg.

> In giving the following pages to the public, it may be proper to state that I am influenced by two motives: a

defence of my own rights, and the rights of Presbyters and Deacons, and a defence of the Church against the usurpations of one of her highest ministers. I conceive that in the following discussion very grave principles, involving the liberty of conscience, and the freedom of Presbyters and Deacons to exercise it, and also the usages and teachings of the Church in this particular, are specially trenched upon by the Bishop. It is with a view of bringing this matter before the Church at large, that, if possible, the question may be settled by such alterations of the law as may make the duty of each order of the ministry plain, that I make the following correspondence public. If a Bishop has a right to introduce prayers into the service of the Church on all occasions of public worship, and keep them there for years, then the Constitution and Canons of the Church need revising, so as to state the fact; and if a Bishop has a right to introduce a mere political opinion into a prayer, by way of simple assertion, by authority of the Church, and to exclude from the exercise of their office all his clergy who do not agree with him, and cannot make the assertion with a good conscience, then the Church herself needs reform.

29. Gillette, *A Few Historic Records*, 120–21.

30. Gillette quoted in WPA, *St. David's Through the Years*, 39–40.

31. Gillette, *A Few Historic Records*, 121–31.

32. WPA, *St. David's Through the Years*, 40–41.

33. Melinda Rankin, *Twenty Years Among the Mexicans, A Narrative of Missionary Labor* (Cincinnati: Chase & Hall, 1875), 97–98.

34. *Twenty Years Among the Mexicans*, 89–90.

35. William Stuart Red. *A History of the Presbyterian Church in Texas* (n.p., 1936), 188.

36. Marten, *Texas Divided*, 75, 175. See also Thaddeus McRae, "Autobiography," typescript, Thaddeus McRae Papers, Barker Texas History Center, University of Texas at Austin; and Webb et al. *Handbook of Texas*, 2:126–27.

37. Daniel, *Southern Protestantism in the Confederacy*, 47.

38. Ted R. Worley, "The Arkansas Peace Society of 1861: A Study in Mountain Unionism," *Journal of Southern History* 24 (Nov. 1958): 455.

39. J. J. Geer, *Beyond the Lines; or, A Yankee Prisoner Loose in Dixie* (Philadelphia: J. W. Daughaday, 1863), 51.

40. *The War of the Rebellion: A Compilation of the Official Records of the Union and Confederate Armies* (*OR*), 1st ser. (Washington: Government Printing Office, 1886), 15:738, 745.

41. Aughey, *Tupelo*. When Aughey first wrote of his experiences, the volume was entitled, *The Iron Furnace; or, Slavery and Secession* (Philadelphia: James S. Claxton, 1863). *Tupelo*, published in 1888, is a later expansion by Aughey of that first work.

42. Aughey, *Tupelo*, 575, 577.

43. *Tupelo*, 579.

44. *Tupelo*, 580–81.

45. *Tupelo*, 583.

46. *Tupelo*, 47. There were several means of dealing with disloyalty in Confederate Mississippi. The state legislatures and civil courts were somewhat effective; the military even more so; but it was the local vigilante groups that were most effective in their attempts to impose conformity. John K. Bettersworth has written that

> one can usually trust the people to provide their own justice when the more refined methods fail. Against dangerous Negroes and persons suspected of disloyalty they formed vigilance committees, conducted trials, and proceeded to hang without much ado. . . . The vigilantes inevitably tended to go to extremes of terrorism and often oppressed their victims relentlessly. In many cases they would take them by surprise, sometimes by the roadside, sometimes at home in the dead of night, in the manner later perfected by the Ku Klux Klan. (*Confederate Mississippi: The People and Policies of a Cotton State in Wartime* [Baton Rouge: Louisiana State University Press, 1943], 41, 254)

47. Aughey, *Tupelo*, 49, 50, 54.

48. *Tupelo*, 110–111.

49. *Tupelo*, 156–57, 221–28.

50. *OR*, 2d ser., 5:128–30.

51. Aughey, *Tupelo*, 520–21.

52. Account of Pelan in *Tupelo*, 69–71. There were clergy members, loyal to the Confederacy, who also lost their lives for

the stances they took. In Jasper and Smith counties, Mississippi, where strong anti-Confederate sentiment existed, loyal "clergymen were being murdered or ordered out of the country; government stores were being seized; bushwhackers were defeating Confederate troops, and the disloyal were threatening to seize the lands of the loyal." Bettersworth, *Confederate Mississippi*, 237.

53. Daniel, *Southern Protestantism in the Confederacy*, 47; information on Lyons in Silver, *Confederate Morale and Church Propaganda*, 19–20.

54. James A. Lyon, "Journal of Rev. James A. Lyon, Columbus, Mississippi, 1861–1870," 24. The original manuscript is privately owned; this writer located a microfilm copy at Rice University, in Houston, Texas.

55. Lyon, "Journal," 58, 98. Lyon's report was published in the *Southern Presbyterian Review* 16 (1863): 1–37. A brief summary of the report can be found in Bettersworth, *Confederate Mississippi*, 304–6.

56. Lyon, "Journal," 30–31. Bettersworth relates that "financially the church suffered greatly in the war. . . . Contributions for salaries of ministers and for church expenses declined greatly. . . . Toward the end of the war financial hardships drove many clergymen to other pursuits for their livelihood. . . . By 1865 there were scarcely half as many clergymen in the state as at the beginning of the war." *Confederate Mississippi*, 296–97.

57. Lyon, "Journal," 30–31. Fast days were often called in the Confederacy as a means of uniting the southern people and gaining religious support for the cause. Defying the orders for the observance of such days was a means some dissidents used to declare their disapproval of secession and war. In Attala County, Mississippi, Joel Harvey announced at Pilgrim's Rest Church that he did not intend to "fast and pray just because Jeff Davis tells me to do so. When they were instigating the war, they didn't call on the churches to pray them into it; and now they needn't call on them to pray 'em out of it." In a statement of true independence, Harvey asserted: "I don't owe allegiance to Jeff Davis or Abe Lincoln." Bettersworth, *Confederate Mississippi*, 223.

58. Lyon, "Journal," 74. On pages 60 through 70 of the "Journal," Lyon gives a rather detailed account of the court-martial and the circumstances surrounding it.

59. Lyon, "Journal," 71–73.

60. "Journal," 75–80.

61. Bettersworth, *Confederate Mississippi*, 306.

62. Lyon, "Journal," 124–29.

63. John K. Bettersworth, "Mississippi Unionism: The Case of the Rev. James A. Lyon," *Journal of Mississippi History* 1 (1939): 52.

64. Charles Elliott, *South-Western Methodism*, 275.

4. Conclusion: The Creative Minority

1. Final quote from Bettersworth, *Confederate Mississippi*, 224.

2. Arnold Toynbee, *A Study of History*, rev. ed. (New York: Oxford University Press, 1972), 161–62.

3. Beringer et al., *Why the South Lost the Civil War*, 101.

4. Two books that address Southern dissent in the wider public are Degler's *The Other South*, and Tatum's *Disloyalty in the Confederacy*.

5. Theodore Parker, *Centenary Edition of the Works of Theodore Parker* (Boston: American Unitarian Association, 1907), 11:279.

6. Paxton Hibben, *Henry Ward Beecher: An American Portrait* (1927; reprint, New York: Press of the Readers Club, 1942), xiv.

7. See David B. Chesebrough, *"God Ordained This War": Sermons on the Sectional Crisis, 1830–1865* (Columbia: University of South Carolina Press, 1991); and Chesebrough, "The Civil War and the Use of Sermons as Historical Documents," *Organization of American Historians Magazine of History* 8 (fall 1993): 26–29.

8. Genovese, *Slaveholders' Dilemma*, 64.

9. Bettersworth, *Confederate Mississippi*, 288.

10. William Lowndes Lipscomb, *A History of Columbus, Mississippi During the 19th Century* (Birmingham, AL: Dispatch Printing Co., 1909), 105–6.

11. Ahlstrom, *A Religious History of the American People*, 672; Beringer et al., *Why the South Lost the Civil War*, 84, 86.

12. Sinclair quoted in Marcus and Burner, *America First-hand*, vol. 2, *From Reconstruction to the Present*, 27.

13. For a more complete accounting of the Caldwell incident from which this information is taken, see Daniel W. Stowell, "'We Have Sinned, and God Has Smitten Us!' John H. Caldwell and

the Religious Meaning of Confederate Defeat," *Georgia Historical Quarterly* 78 (spring 1994): 1–38.

14. Dallas Lee, *The Cotton Patch Evidence* (New York: Harper & Row, 1971), 7–8.

15. *Cotton Patch Evidence*, 37–38, 105–42.

16. *Cotton Patch Evidence*, 67–85, 124, 143–44.

Davis, Reuben. *Recollections of Mississippi and Mississippians.* 1889.

Bibliography

Nineteenth-Century Sources

Books

Armstrong, George D. *The Christian Doctrine of Slavery.* New York: Charles Scribner, 1857.

Aughey, John H. *The Iron Furnace; or, Slavery and Secession.* Philadelphia: James S. Claxton, 1863.

———. *Tupelo.* Lincoln, NE: State Journal Co., 1888.

Bassett, John S. *Slavery in North Carolina.* Baltimore: Johns Hopkins University Press, 1899.

Booth, William A. *The Writings of William A. Booth, M.D. During the Controversy upon Slavery.* Somerville, TN: Reeves and Yancy, 1845.

Broadus, John A. *Memoir of James Petigru Boyce, D.D., LL.D.* New York: A. C. Armstrong and Son, 1893.

Brownlow, William G. *The Great Iron Wheel Examined or, Its False Spokes Extracted, and an Exhibition of Elder Graves, its Builder. In a Series of Chapters.* Nashville: Brownlow, 1856.

———. *Helps to the Study of Presbyterianism or an Unsophisticated Exposition of Calvinism, with a view to a more easy Interpretation of the Same. To Which is added a Brief Account of the Life and Travels of the Author, Interspersed with Anecdotes.* Knoxville: F. S. Heiskell Co., 1834.

———. *Sketches of the Rise, Progress, and Decline of Secession.* Philadelphia: George Childs, 1862.

Caruthers, Eli Washington. *The Life of David Caldwell.* Greensboro, NC: Swaim & Sherwood, 1842.

Caskey, Thomas W. *Caskey's Last Book, Containing an Autobiographical Sketch of His Ministerial Life, With Essays and Sermons.* Edited by B. F. Manire. Nashville: Messenger Publishing Co., 1896.

Cuthbert, James H. *Life of Richard Fuller, D.D.* New York: Sheldon and Co., 1879.

Reprint, with an introduction by William D. McCain and preface by Laura D. S. Harrell, Hattiesburg: University and College Press of Mississippi, 1972.

Elliott, Charles. *South-Western Methodism: A History of the Methodist Episcopal Church in the South-West from 1844 to 1864.* Edited by LeRoy M. Vernon. Cincinnati: Poe & Hitchcock, 1868.

Fee, John Gregg. *Autobiography of John G. Fee, Berea, Kentucky.* Chicago: National Christian Assoc., 1891.

Feemster, Zemas E. *The Traveling Refugee; or The Curse and Cure of the Rebellion in the United States.* Springfield, MA: Steam Press of Baker & Phillips, 1865.

Fuller, Richard, and Francis Wayland. *Domestic Slavery Considered as a Scriptural Institution.* New York: Lewis Colby, 1845.

Geer, J. J. *Beyond the Lines; or A Yankee Prisoner Loose in Dixie.* Philadelphia: J. W. Daughaday, 1863.

Gillette, Charles. *A Few Historic Records of the Church in the Diocese of Texas, During the Rebellion.* New York: John A. Gray & Green, 1865.

Goodloe, Daniel R. *The Southern Platform: or, Manual of Southern Sentiment on the Subject of Slavery.* Boston: John P. Jewett & Co., 1858.

Graves, J. R. *The Great Iron Wheel; or, Republicanism Backwards and Christianity Reversed.* 17th ed. Nashville: Graves, Marks, and Rulland, 1856.

Helper, Hinton Rowan. *The Impending Crisis of the South: How to Meet It.* New York: A. B. Burdick, 1860.

Hersey, John. *Appeal to Christians on the Subject of Slavery.* 3d ed. Baltimore: Sherwood and Co., n.d.

Janney, Samuel H. *Memoirs.* Philadelphia: Friends Book Assoc., 1881.

Marine, F. E. *Sketch of Reverend John Hersey, Minister of the Gospel of the M.E. Church.* Baltimore: Hoffman & Co., 1879.

Matlock, L. C. *The Antislavery Struggle and Triumph in the Methodist Episcopal Church.* New York: Phillips & Hunt, 1881.

Nichols, George. *The Story of the Great March.* New York: Harper and Brothers, 1865.

Ought American Slavery to be Perpetuated? A Debate Between Rev. W. G. Brownlow and Rev. A. Pryne, held at Philadelphia, 1858. Philadelphia: J. B. Lippincott & Co., 1858.

Palmer, Benjamin Morgan. *The Life and Letters of James Henley Thornwell.* Richmond, VA: Whittet & Shepperson, 1875.

Paxton, J. D. *Letters on Slavery Addressed to the Cumberland Con-*

gregation, Virginia. Lexington, KY: Abraham T. Skillman, 1833.

Pendleton, James Madison. *Reminiscences of a Long Life*. Louisville, KY: Baptist Book Concern, 1891.

Priest, Josiah. *Bible Defense of Slavery: and Origin, Fortunes and History of the Negro Race*. Glasgow, KY: W. S. Brown, M.D., 1852.

Rankin, Melinda. *Twenty Years Among the Mexicans, A Narrative of Missionary Labor*. Cincinnati: Chase and Hall, 1875.

Ross, Frederick A. *Slavery Ordained of God*. Philadelphia: J. B. Lippincott & Co., 1859.

Smith, George G. *The Life and Letters of James Osgood Andrew, Bishop of the Methodist Episcopal Church, South*. Nashville: Southern Methodist Publishing House, 1883.

Smith, Wesley. *A Defense of the Methodist Episcopal Church Against the Charges of Rev. S. Kelley and Others*. Fairmont, VA: Western Virginia Republican Office, 1855.

Stanton, Robert Livingston. *The Church and the Rebellion: A Consideration of the Rebellion Against the Government of the United States; and the Agency of the Church, North and South, in Relation Thereto*. New York: Derby & Miller, 1864.

Temple, Oliver P. *East Tennessee and the Civil War*. Cincinnati: Robert Clarke Co., 1899.

The War of the Rebellion: A Compilation of the Official Records of the Union and Confederate Armies. 128 parts in 70 vols. Washington: Government Printing Office, 1880–1901.

Weeks, Stephen B. *Southern Quakers and Slavery*. Baltimore: Johns Hopkins University Press, 1896.

Sermons

Atkinson, Thomas. *On the Causes of our National Troubles. A Sermon delivered in St. James Church, Wilmington, N.C., on Friday, the 4th of January, 1861*. Wilmington, NC: Herald Book and Jobs Office, 1861.

Boyd, Andrew H. H. *Thanksgiving Sermon, delivered in Winchester, Virginia, on Thursday, 29th November, 1860*. Winchester: Winchester Virginian, 1860.

Breckinridge, Robert J. "The Union to be Preserved." In *Fast Day Sermons*, 98–126.

Brownlow, William G. *A Sermon on Slavery: A Vindication of the Methodist Church, South: Her Position Stated*. Knoxville, TN:

Kinsloe & Rice, 1857.

Bushnell, Horace. *A Discourse on the Slavery Question.* Hartford, CT: Case Library, 1839.

Caldwell, John H. *Slavery and Southern Methodism: Two Sermons Preached in the Methodist Church in Newnan, Georgia.* New York: Caldwell, 1865.

Clapp, Theodore. *Slavery.* New Orleans: John Gibson, 1838.

Clough, Simon. *A Candid Appeal to the Citizens of the United States.* New York: A. K. Bertran, 1834.

Cuthbert, Lucius, Jr. *The Scriptural Grounds for Secession From the Union.* Charleston, SC: Welch, Harris & Co., 1861.

Dabney, Robert Lewis. *The Christian's Best Motive for Patriotism.* Richmond, VA: Chas. H. Wynn, 1860.

Dalzell, W. T. D. *A Sermon.* San Antonio: Herald Book and Job Press, 1863.

Dunaway, Thomas. *A Sermon.* Richmond, VA: Enquirer Book and Job Press, 1864.

Dunwoody, Samuel. *A Sermon on the Subject of Slavery.* Columbia, SC: S. Weir, 1837.

Fast Day Sermons; or The Pulpit on the State of the Country. New York: Rudd & Carleton, 1861.

Fuller, Richard. *Address Before the American Colinization Society.* Baltimore: Office of the Trust Union, 1851.

Gregg, Alexander. *The Duties Growing Out of It, and the Benefits to be Expected From the Present War.* Austin: State Gazette Job Office, 1861.

———. *Primary Charge to the Clergy of the Protestant Episcopal Church in the Diocese of Texas.* Austin: State Gazette Job Office, 1863.

———. *A Sermon.* Austin: Texas Almanac Office, 1862.

———. *A Sermon.* Austin: Texas Almanac Office, 1863.

Hamilton, W. T. *Duties of Masters and Slaves Respectively; or, Domestic Slavery as Sanctioned by the Bible.* Mobile, AL: F. H. Brooks, 1844.

Junkin, George. *The Integrity of Our National Union.* Cincinnati: R. P. Donogh, 1843.

Longstreet, Augustus Baldwin. *Fast-Day Sermon.* Columbia, SC: Townsend & North, 1861.

Lord, W. W. *A Discourse in Honor of Capt. Paul Hamilton.* Vicksburg, MS: M. Shannon, 1863.

Miles, James W. *God in History.* Charleston: Evans & Cogswell, 1863.

Palmer, Benjamin Morgan. *A Discourse Before the General Assembly of South Carolina*. Columbia, SC: Charles P. Pelham, State Printer, 1864.

———. "Slavery a Divine Trust: Duty of the South to Preserve and Perpetuate It." In *Fast Day Sermons*, 57–80.

Paris, John. *Funeral Discourse*. Greensborough, NC: A. W. Ingold & Co., 1864.

Pierce, George Foster. *Sermon*. Milledgeville, GA: Groughton, Nisbet, and Barnes, 1863.

Pierce, H. N. *Sermon Preached in St. John's Church, Mobile, on the 13th of June, 1861, the National Fast Appointed by His Excellency Jefferson Davis, President of the Confederate States of America*. Mobile, AL: Farrow & Dennett, 1861.

Pinckney, Charles Cotesworth. *Nebuchadnezzar's Fault and Fall*. Charleston, SC: A. J. Burke, 1861.

Porter, Charles. *Our Country's Danger and Security*. Utica, NY: R. W. Roberts, 1844.

Prentiss, William O. *A Sermon Preached at St. Peter's Church, Charleston, by the Rev. William O. Prentiss, on Wednesday, November 21, 1860, being a Day of Public Fasting, Humiliation and Prayer*. Charleston: Evans & Cogswell, 1860.

Rees, W. A. *A Sermon on Divine Providence*. Austin: Texas Almanac Office, 1863.

Stiles, Joseph. *National Rectitude the Only True Basis of National Prosperity: An Appeal to the Confederate States*. Petersburg, VA: Evangelical Tract Society, 1863.

Thornwell, James Henley. "Our National Sins." In *Fast Day Sermons*, 9–56.

———. *The Rights and the Duties of Masters*. Charleston, SC: Walker and James, 1850.

Tichenor, Isaac T. *Fast Day Sermon*. Montgomery, AL: Montgomery Advertiser Book and Jobs Printing Office, 1863.

Tracey, Joseph. *Natural Equality*. Windsor, VT: Chronicle Press, 1833.

Vedder, C. S. *Offer Unto God Thanksgiving*. Charleston, SC: Evans & Cogswell, 1861.

Wightman, John T. *The Glory of God, the Defense of the South*. Charleston, SC: Evans & Cogswell, 1861.

Wilson, Joseph R. *Mutual Relations of Masters and Slaves as Taught in the Bible*. Augusta, GA: Steam Power Press of Chronicle and Sentinel, 1861.

Winkler, Edwin T. *Duties of the Christian Soldier*. Charleston, SC: A. J. Burke, 1861.

Newspapers, Periodicals, and Other Publications

Alabama Baptist, Dec. 6, 1845.

Knoxville Whig, May 18, 1861.

Liberator, Jan. 1, 1831.

Lyon, James A. "Religious Instruction of Slaves." *Southern Presbyterian Review* 16 (1863): 1–37.

Minutes of the Savannah River Association, Held at Bluffton Baptist Church, November 18, 1860. N.p., Savannah River Assoc., 1860.

Minutes of the State Convention of the Baptist Denomination in South Carolina, at its Twenty-Fourth Anniversary held at Darlington Baptist Church, commencing on the 7th and ending on the 10th of December. N.p., n.d.

Minutes of the Thirty-Eighth Annual Session of the Alabama State Convention, Held at Tuskegee, November 9–13, 1860. Tuskegee, AL: Office of the South Western Baptist, 1860.

Minutes of the Twenty-Fifth Anniversary of the Chickasaw Baptist Association. Sept. 16–18, 1864. Meredian, MS: Clarion Book and Job Office, 1865.

Mississippi Baptist, Jan. 3, 1861.

North Carolina Presbyterian, Nov. 26, 1859.

Proceedings of the Southern Baptist Convention, May 10–13, 1861. Richmond: MacFarlane and Fergusson, 1861.

Richmond Enquirer, Sept. 29, 1835; Dec. 18, 1860.

Southern Baptist and General Intelligencer, Oct. 9, 1835.

Southern Episcopalian, Dec. 1860.

Southern Presbyterian, Mar. 9, 1861.

Thornwell, James Henley. "Critical Notices." *Southern Presbyterian Review* 4 (Jan. 1851): 452.

Manuscripts

Lyon, James A. "Journal of Rev. James A. Lyon, Columbus, Mississippi, 1861–1870." Dept. of Archives and History, Jackson, MS. (Original manuscript is privately owned, but typewritten and microfilm copies can be found at the Mississippi Dept. of Archives and History, as well as Rice University, Houston, TX.)

McRae, Thaddeus. Papers. Barker Texas History Center, University of Texas at Austin.

Twentieth-Century Sources

Books

Ahlstrom, Sydney E. *A Religious History of the American People.* New Haven, CT: Yale University Press, 1972.

Basler, Roy P., ed. *The Collected Works of Abraham Lincoln.* 9 vols. New Brunswick, NJ: Rutgers University Press, 1953.

Beales, Carleton. *War Within a War: The Confederacy Against Itself.* Philadelphia: Chilton Books, 1965.

Beringer, Richard E., Herman Hattaway, Archer Jones, and William N. Still, Jr. *Why the South Lost the Civil War.* Athens: University of Georgia Press, 1986.

Bettersworth, John K. *Confederate Mississippi: The People and Policies of a Cotton State in Wartime.* Baton Rouge: Louisiana State University Press, 1943.

———. "The Home Front, 1861–1865." In *A History of Mississippi*, edited by Richard A. McLemore. Vol. 1. Hattiesburg: University and College Press of Mississippi, 1973.

Bodo, John R. *The Protestant Clergy and Public Issues, 1812–1848.* Princeton, NJ: Princeton University Press, 1954.

Boyd, Jesse L. *A Popular History of the Baptists in Mississippi.* Jackson, MS: Baptist Banner Press, 1930.

Brock, Peter. *The Quaker Peace Testimony 1660 to 1914.* York, Eng.: Sessions Book Trust, 1990.

Burtis, Mary E. *Moncure Conway.* New Brunswick, NJ: Rutgers University Press, 1952.

Channing, Steven A. *Crisis of Fear: Secession in South Carolina.* New York: Simon and Schuster, 1970.

Chesebrough, David B. *"God Ordained This War": Sermons on the Sectional Crisis, 1830–1865.* Columbia: University of South Carolina Press, 1991.

Chestnut, Mary Boykin. *A Diary from Dixie.* Foreword by Edmund Wilson. Edited by Ben Ames Wilson. Cambridge: Harvard University Press, 1980.

Conway, Moncure Daniel. *Autobiography, Memories and Experiences of Moncure Daniel Conway.* 2 vols. Boston: Houghton Mifflin, 1904.

Coulter, E. Merton. *William G. Brownlow: Fighting Parson of the Southern Highlands.* Chapel Hill: University of North Carolina Press, 1937.

Current, Richard Nelson. *Lincoln's Loyalists: Union Soldiers from the Confederacy.* New York: Oxford University Press, 1992.

Daniel, W. Harrison. *Southern Protestantism in the Confederacy.* Bedford, VA: Print Shop, 1989.

Davis, T. Frederick. *History of Jacksonville, Florida and Vicinity.* St. Augustine, FL: Record Co., 1925.

Davis, William Watson. *The Civil War and Reconstruction in Florida.* Gainesville: University of Florida Press, 1964.

Degler, Carl N. *The Other South: Southern Dissenters in the Nineteenth Century.* New York: Harper & Row, 1974.

Eaton, Clement. *Freedom of Thought in the Old South.* Durham, NC: Duke University Press, 1940.

Escott, Paul D. *After Secession: Jefferson Davis and the Failure of Confederate Nationalism.* Baton Rouge: Louisiana State University Press, 1978.

Faust, Drew Gilpin. *The Creation of Confederate Nationalism: Ideology and Identity in the Civil War South.* Baton Rouge: Louisiana State University Press, 1988.

————. *A Sacred Circle: The Dilemma of the Intellectual in the Old South, 1840–1860.* Baltimore: John Hopkins University Press, 1977.

Genovese, Eugene D. *The Slaveholders' Dilemma: Freedom and Progress in Southern Conservative Thought, 1820–1860.* Columbia: University of South Carolina Press, 1992.

Goen, C. C. *Broken Churches, Broken Nation.* Macon, GA: Mercer University Press, 1985.

Grayson, William J. *Witness to Sorrow: The Antebellum Autobiography of William J. Grayson.* Columbia: University of South Carolina Press, 1990.

Hamilton, Joseph G. de Roulhac. *Reconstruction in North Carolina.* 1914. Reprint, Freeport, NY: Books for Libraries Press, 1971.

Heathcote, Charles W. *The Lutheran Church and the Civil War.* Chicago: Fleming H. Revell, 1949.

Hibben, Paxton. *Henry Ward Beecher: An American Portrait.* Foreword by Sinclair Lewis. 1927. Reprint, New York: Press of the Readers Club, 1942.

Hochling, A. A. *Last Train from Atlanta.* New York: Thomas Yoseloff, 1958.

Johnson, Thomas C. *The Life and Letters of Robert Lewis Dabney.* 1903. Reprint, Edinburgh: Banner of Truth Trust, 1977.

Klingberg, Frank W. *The Southern Claims Commission.* Berkeley:

University of California Press, 1955.

Lander, Ernest M., Jr., and Robert K. Ackerman. *Perspectives in South Carolina History: The First 300 Years*. Columbia: University of South Carolina Press, 1973.

Lee, Dallas. *The Cotton Patch Evidence*. New York: Harper & Row, 1971.

Leverett, Rudy H. *Legend of the Free State of Jones*. Jackson: University and College Press of Mississippi, 1984.

Lipscomb, William Lowndes. *A History of Columbus, Mississippi During the 19th Century*. Birmingham, AL: Dispatch Printing Co., 1909.

Loveland, Anne C. *Southern Evangelicals and the Social Order, 1800–1860*. Baton Rouge: Louisiana State University Press, 1980.

McCash, William B. *Thomas R. R. Cobb (1823–1862): The Making of a Southern Nationalist*. Macon, GA: Mercer University Press, 1983.

McPherson, James M. *Battle Cry of Freedom: The Civil War Era*. New York: Oxford University Press, 1988.

Marcus, Robert T., and David Burner. *America Firsthand*. 2 vols. New York: St. Martin's Press, 1989.

Marten, James. *Texas Divided: Loyalty and Dissent in the Lone Star State, 1856–1874*. Lexington: University Press of Kentucky, 1990.

Matthews, Donald G. *Religion in the Old South*. Chicago: University of Chicago Press, 1977.

Nevins, Allen. *Ordeal of the Union*. 2 vols. New York: Charles Scribner's, 1947.

Nicholson, Roy S. *Wesleyan Methodism in the South*. Syracuse, NY: Wesleyan Methodist Publishing House, 1933.

Obear, Katherine Theus. *Through the Years in Old Winnsboro*. 1940. Reprint, Spartanburg, SC: Reprint Co., 1980.

Parker, Theodore. *Centenary Edition of the Works of Theodore Parker*. 15 vols. Boston: American Unitarian Assoc., 1907.

Potter, David. *The Impending Crisis, 1848–1861*. New York: Harper & Row, 1976.

Rainwater, Perry L. *Mississippi, Storm Center of Secession*. Baton Rouge: Otto Claiton, 1938.

Red, William Stuart. *A History of the Presbyterian Church in Texas*. N.p., 1936.

Robert, Joseph Clarke. *The Road to Monticello: A Study of the Virginia Slavery Debate of 1832*. Durham, NC: Duke University Press, 1941.

Scarborough, Ruth. *The Opposition to Slavery in Georgia Prior to 1860*. Nashville: George Peabody College for Teachers, 1933.

Silver, James W. *Confederate Morale and Church Propaganda*. New York: Norton, 1957.

Sitterson, Joseph Carlyle. *The Secession Movement in North Carolina*. Chapel Hill: University of North Carolina Press, 1939.

Smith, H. Sheldon. *In His Image, but . . . Racism in Southern Religion*. Durham, NC: Duke University Press, 1972.

Snay, Mitchell. *Gospel of Disunion: Religion and Separatism in the Antebellum South*. Cambridge: Cambridge University Press, 1993.

Sweet, William Warren. *The Methodist Episcopal Church and the Civil War*. Cincinnati: Methodist Book Concern Press, 1912.

———. *The Story of Religion in America*. New York: Harper Brothers, 1950.

Sydnor, Charles S. *The Development of Southern Sectionalism, 1819–1848*. Baton Rouge: Louisiana State University Press, 1934.

Tatum, Georgia Lee. *Disloyalty in the Confederacy*. Chapel Hill: University of North Carolina Press, 1934.

Thomas, Albert Sidney. *A Historical Account of the Protestant Episcopal Church in South Carolina*. Columbia, SC: R. L. Bryan, 1957.

Thomas, Emory M. *The Confederate Nation, 1861–1865*. New York: HarperCollins, 1979.

Thompson, Ernest Trice. *Presbyterians in the South*. 2 vols. Richmond, VA: John Knox Press, 1963.

Tise, Larry E. *Proslavery: A History of the Defense of Slavery in America, 1701–1840*. Athens: University of Georgia Press, 1987.

Toynbee, Arnold. *A Study of History*. Rev. ed. New York: Oxford University Press, 1972.

Vander Velde, Lewis George. *The Presbyterian Churches and the Federal Union, 1861–1869*. Cambridge: Harvard University Press, 1932.

Webb, Walter P. et al., eds. *The Handbook of Texas*. 2 vols. Austin: Texas State Historical Assoc., 1952.

Wilson, Charles Reagan, ed. *Religion in the South*. Jackson: University and College Press of Mississippi, 1985.

Wood, Forest G. *The Arrogance of Faith: Christianity and Race in America from the Colonial Era to the Twentieth Century*. New York: Alfred A. Knopf, 1990.

Works Projects Administration (WPA). *St. David's Through the Years*. Austin: Betty Gilmer Chapter of St. David's Guild, 1942.

Wright, Edward Needles. *Conscientious Objectors in the Civil War*.

1931. Reprint, New York: A. S. Barnes & Co., 1961.
Zuber, Richard L. *Jonathan Worth: A Biography of a Southern Unionist.* Chapel Hill: University of North Carolina Press, 1965.

Unpublished Dissertations

Dodd, Donald Bradford. "Unionism in Confederate Alabama." Ph.D. diss., University of Georgia, 1969.
Hickin, Patricia P. "Antislavery in Virginia, 1831–1861." Ph.D. diss., University of Virginia, 1968.

Articles and Newspapers

Bettersworth, John K. "Mississippi Unionism: The Case of the Rev. James A. Lyon." *Journal of Mississippi History* 1 (1939): 37–52.
Buengner, Walter L. "Texas and the Riddle of Secession." *Southwestern Historical Quarterly* 87 (Oct. 1983): 151–82.
Chesebrough, David B. "The Civil War and the Use of Sermons as Historical Documents." *Organization of American Historians Magazine of History* 8 (fall 1993): 26–29.
———. "Dissenting Clergy in Confederate Mississippi." *Journal of Mississippi History* 55 (summer 1993): 115–31.
"Clarence Jordan." *Christian Century,* Nov. 12, 1969, 1442.
Daniel, W. Harrison. "Protestantism and Patriotism in the Confederacy." *Mississippi Quarterly* 24 (spring 1971): 117–34.
———. "The Southern Baptists in the Confederacy." *Civil War History* 6 (1960): 389–401.
DesChamps, Margaret B. "Benjamin Morgan Palmer, Orator-Preacher of the Confederacy." *Southern Speech Journal* 19 (Sept. 1953): 14–22.
Doherty, Herbert J. "Union Nationalism in Georgia." *Georgia Historical Quarterly* 37 (Mar. 1953): 18–38.
Eaton, Clement. "Mob Violence in the Old South." *Mississippi Valley Historical Review* 29 (Dec. 1942): 351–70.
Embree, Edwin Rogers. "A Kentucky Crusader." *American Mercury* 24 (Sept. 1931): 98–107.
Fisher, Noel. "'The Leniency Shown Them Has Been Unavailing': The Confederate Occupation of East Tennessee." *Civil War History* 40 (Dec. 1994): 275–91.
Hamilton, Joseph G. de Roulhac. "Heroes of America." *Publications of the Southern History Association* 11 (Jan. 1907): 10–19.

Johnson, Clifton H. "Abolitionist Missionary Activities in North Carolina." *North Carolina Historical Review* 40 (July 1963): 295–320.

Kibler, Lillian A. "Unionist Sentiment in South Carolina." *Journal of Southern History* 4 (Aug. 1938): 346–66.

Liberator, Jan. 1, 1931.

Long, Durwood. "Unanimity and Disloyalty in Secessionist Alabama." *Civil War History* 11 (Sept. 1965): 257–73.

Maddox, Jack P., Jr. "Proslavery Millennialism: Social Eschatology in Antebellum Southern Calvinism." *American Quarterly* 31 (spring 1979): 46–62.

Monroe, Haskell. "Southern Presbyterians and the Secession Crisis." *Civil War History* 6 (1960): 351–60.

Moore, Edmund A. "Robert J. Breckinridge and the Slavery Aspect of the Presbyterian Schism of 1837." *Church History* 4 (Dec. 1935): 282–94.

Norton, Wesley. "The Methodist Episcopal Church and the Civil Disturbances in North Texas in 1859 and 1860." *Southwestern Historical Quarterly* 68 (Jan. 1965): 317–41.

Owsley, Frank L. "Defeatism in the Confederacy." *North Carolina Historical Review* 3 (July 1926): 446–56.

Raper, Horace W. "William W. Holden and the Peace Movement in North Carolina." *North Carolina Historical Review* 31 (Oct. 1954): 493–516.

Roberts, A. Sellew. "The Peace Movement in North Carolina." *Mississippi Valley Historical Review* 11 (Sept. 1924): 190–99.

Shanks, Henry T. "Disloyalty to the Confederacy in Southwestern Virginia, 1861–1865." *North Carolina Historical Review* 21 (Apr. 1944): 118–35.

Smyrl, Frank N. "Unionism in Texas, 1856–1861." *Southwestern Historical Quarterly* 68 (Oct. 1964): 172–95.

Stowell, Daniel W. "'We Have Sinned, and God Has Smitten Us!' John H. Caldwell and the Religious Meaning of Confederate Defeat." *Georgia Historical Quarterly* 78 (spring 1994): 1–38.

Tolbert, Noble J. "Daniel Worth: Tar Heel Abolitionist." *North Carolina Historical Review* 39 (summer 1962): 284–304.

Westerkamp, Marilyn J. "James Henley Thornwell, Pro-Slavery Spokesman with a Calvinist Faith." *South Carolina Historical Magazine* 87 (Jan. 1986): 49–64.

Wight, Willard E. "The Churches and the Confederate Cause." *Civil War History* 6 (1960): 361–73.

Wooster, Ralph A. "An Analysis of the Membership of the Texas Secession Convention." *Southwestern Historical Quarterly* 62 (Jan. 1959): 322–35.

Worley, Ted R. "The Arkansas Peace Society of 1861: A Study in Mountain Unionism." *Journal of Southern History* 24 (Nov. 1958): 445–57.

Index

abolitionism: atheism and, 20; northern religion and, 8–9; threat to southern way of life, 8
Amana Colony, 59
American Colonization Society, 31
"American Slavery and the Immediate Duty of Slave-holders" (Caruthers), 65
Andrew, James O., 4, 51
Appeal to Christians on the Subject of Slavery (Hersey), 41–42
Arkansas Peace Society, 73
Atkinson, Thomas, 17
Aughey, John H., 74–78, 92, 99

Baptists, schism of 1845, 5
Beauregard, P. G. T., 73–74
Beecher, Henry Ward, 45, 89
Benjamin, Judah P., 56
Berea College, 45
Bewley, Anthony, 34–37, 49, 91
Blount, "Parson," 33–34, 49, 91
Booth, William G., 4
Boyd, Andrew H. H., 15
Boyd, Frederick W., 79–80
Branum, Solomon, 73
Breckinridge, Robert J., 43–44
Brewer, Aaron G., 22
Brisbane, William Henry, 31–33, 49, 91
Brown, John, 45
Brownlow, William G., 1–2, 52–56, 91
Bushnell, Horace, 9
Butler, James A., 21–22

Caldwell, John H., 95–96

Calhoun, John C., 5
Carithers, John H., 73
Carothers, Eli Washington, 64–65, 91
Carter, William B., 56–57, 90
Caskey, Thomas, 5–6
Christadelphians, 59
"Christian's Best Motive For Patriotism, The" (Dabney), 22–23
Churchill, Orin, 63
Clapp, Theodore, 10
Clark, John T., 62
Clay, Henry, 5
clergymen: financial hardship in war, 155n. 56; loyalty and, 21–22; persecution of loyal, 114–15n. 52; prolonging the war, 26–27; reflectors or molders, 88–89; secession and, 22
Clough, Simon, 8–9
Cobb, Thomas R. R., 17
colonization, 31, 43
Confederacy: formation of, 50; suppression of dissent in, 50–51
conformity, 25–26; enforcing, 37–38
conscientious objectors, 59–60
Conway, Moncure Daniel, 46–48, 49, 59, 91
creative minority, hope of civilization, 87, 100

Dabney, Robert Lewis, 22–23, 37, 106–7n. 35
Davis, H. W., 73
Davis, Jefferson, conscientious

DAVID B. CHESEBROUGH is the assistant chair in the Department of History at Illinois State University. He has published two previous books on religion and the sectional crisis: *"God Ordained This War": Sermons on the Sectional Crisis, 1830–1865* and *"No Sorrow Like Our Sorrow": Northern Protestant Ministers and the Assassination of Lincoln.*